3/6/19
#25.00

D0648603

On Being 40(ish)

EDITED BY

Lindsey Mead

Simon & Schuster

NEW YORK LONDON TORONTO SYDNEY NEW DELHI

Simon & Schuster
1230 Avenue of the Americas
New York, NY 10020

First Simon & Schuster hardcover edition February 2019

SIMON & SCHUSTER and colophon are registered trademarks of Simon & Schuster, Inc.

For information about special discounts for bulk purchases, please contact
Simon & Schuster Special Sales at 1-866-506-1949 or business@simonandschuster.com.

The Simon & Schuster Speakers Bureau can bring authors to your live event.
For more information or to book an event, contact the Simon & Schuster Speakers Bureau
at 1-866-248-3049 or visit our website at www.simonspeakers.com.

Interior design by Ruth Lee-Mui

Manufactured in the United States of America

1   3   5   7   9   10   8   6   4   2

Library of Congress Cataloging-in-Publication Data

Names: Mead, Lindsey.
Title: On being 40(ish) / edited by Lindsey Mead.
Description: New York : Simon & Schuster, [2018]
Identifiers: LCCN 2017061050| ISBN 9781501172120 (hardcover) | ISBN
9781501172144 (trade paper) | ISBN 9781501172137 (e-book)
Subjects: LCSH: Women—United States—Biography.
Classification: LCC CT3260 .P74 2019 | DDC 920.720973—dc23
LC record available at https://lccn.loc.gov/2017061050

ISBN 978-1-5011-7212-0
ISBN 978-1-5011-7213-7 (ebook)

For all women in the prime of their lives

The pure feelings one had in adult life were complicated and mitigated, and they were dearly paid for, but worth everything they cost.

—LAURIE COLWIN

Contents

Introduction

LINDSEY MEAD

I sat on the rickety wooden steps that descended from Courtney's house to the beach, watching the sky's riotous colors as the sun set over Chappaquiddick, the tiny island that floats off the eastern edge of Martha's Vineyard. The sky above swirled with a particularly brilliant blend of orange and pink. The evening had grown chillier as the sun went down, and I pulled my thin Patagonia fleece jacket more tightly around me. As the colors faded, I turned back to the house, which glowed, a glass box built into the spectacular landscape.

Through the large window that fronted the ocean, I

could see some of my dearest friends sitting together on couches, and their animated voices and laughter carried out, calling me back into the cozy living room. As I pushed the heavy glass door open and stepped onto the concrete floor, I heard Allison's voice. "This really has been the best decade yet." I walked quietly into the circle and sat down next to Quincy on the edge of one of the couches. The room smelled of the ginger and soy sauce that flavored the salmon that was in the oven. Courtney was an excellent cook, and by this night, the final of our three-day weekend, we'd noted that her early post-college years in Tokyo had shaped her culinary tastes.

I could feel the cold of my feet through my jeans as I tucked them underneath me. I looked around the room at my dearest friends splayed on couches and chairs. There were six of us this year, on our seventh annual weekend reunion. In 2010 Allison and Kathryn had started this tradition, and since then we'd gathered, always in late September, at homes from Florida to Rhode Island to Lake Tahoe. The weekend had become sacrosanct to me—I'd never missed one.

"At least so far I love this decade. I am surprised, honestly, but it feels that way." Allison went on, and I glanced around the dusky room at the familiar faces that I had known since we met at Princeton, at eighteen. Now, in our early forties, we had officially passed the "we've been friends with each other more than half of our lives" mark.

Several others nodded. "I thought of forty as so old. Forty was my parents when I was a kid. But now it's me, and it's actually sort of great," Courtney said from her perch across from me.

"I have such vivid memories of my dad turning forty," I broke in. "Mum gave him a Windsurfer. We had a party in the backyard. Hilary and I greeted people, and I remember the picture that Mum took of him with his two girls and the Windsurfer in the background."

It is often the case that I'm not totally sure where my memories end and the photos that I've seen so many times begin. I don't know exactly why this is, but I suspect it has something to do with how throughout my childhood I frequently and carefully pored over the photo albums my father made and kept, each meticulously annotated in his fountain pen script. But for whatever reason, I do recall my father's fortieth birthday party with particular clarity, though I wonder now if it was that I somehow had a sense of the significance of the milestone, even then. I can imagine his face, with the mustache he wore for most of my childhood, smiling at the guests, and the Windsurfer my mother gave him tipped up against the back wall of our house.

"And then there's that thing when you see someone from college," Quincy said. "And you remember them as they were, but obviously we're not that anymore." I started laughing quietly as Courtney stood up and walked back to her bedroom.

"That happened to me at work recently," I added. "I saw Jamie, and my God, he's all senior now, and he walked into a conference room in a high-rise, and all I could think about was how the last time I saw him he was facedown in a taproom, you know?" More knowing laughter, and then Leonora leaned forward.

"That feels especially real when I look at the old photos you used to reprint for us, Linds."

"Remember when you had to wait twenty-four hours— or sometimes, if you were really lucky, only one, for photos to be developed?" I said, suddenly laughing hard.

"Yup, and it's when I look back at those pictures that I'm most aware of how everyone has grown up."

We all looked up as Courtney walked back into the room, carrying an eight-by-ten framed photo.

"Remember this?" she said, holding out the frame. I stood up and looked over at the photograph she held. I knew it well. It was a large group of us at the P-rade during reunions weekend, right before we graduated. We were wearing our canvas Princeton reunion jackets and, I remember, drinking warm, flat beer from a case that was sitting behind us on the grassy hill.

We look so young, of course. But we also look unabashedly jubilant, and I remember a distinct feeling that the future rippled out in front of us, assured, shimmering, certain. I have so many similar pictures like that one at the P-rade from our years at college. Our hair is too long, our faces are beer-puffy, and we are usually wearing, to a person, an unflattering uniform of baggy jeans, oversize plaid flannel shirts, and baseball caps. We are often holding red Solo cups, which inevitably were filled with cheap beer or vodka and whatever mixer we could rustle up. The days of plaid and Solo cups feel simultaneously like yesterday and like a different life.

Back then we talked endlessly about everything. The future was out there, and sometimes we imagined it, but we were also concerned with the minutiae of our everyday lives in that moment. We discussed ad nauseam what boy was interested in what girl, who was going to house parties with who, where we should go on an empty Saturday afternoon to lie in the sun (the horrors of that particular dilemma are etched on my skin now, believe me). We talked about grades and school, and I've often thought that the fact that I can tell you what each of my dear college friends wrote her senior thesis on is some kind of unusual marker of intimacy.

In the years after college, we fanned out, mostly to New York, San Francisco, and Boston, where we crammed into small apartments, often together, and into business suits and heels. Then, on our first, clunky cell phones, we talked about work and travel and asked questions about Excel and when being drunk became worrisome. I remember vividly a conversation I had with Quincy. I stood in my tiny bathroom in my first apartment in Beacon Hill packing for yet another business trip in my first job as a management consultant while she regaled me with a story about her first kiss the night before with the man she's now been married to for fourteen years. As the years unfolded we began wondering about who we'd marry, children we might have, and what we were going to grow up to be.

Now that we are in our forties, many of the questions that preoccupied us in earlier decades are answered. That's both wonderful and sorrowful, of course, because with answers come closed doors. What we worry about now is totally different. Almost everyone in this particular group of friends has children, so we talk, and worry, about them a lot. We worry about our aging parents and their health. We worry about wrinkles and whether it's okay at this age to be intrigued by the clothes at Talbots and even—gasp—Chico's. Too drapey? We worry about our marriages and about our careers and those of our partners. Many of the questions feel bigger, and they're certainly more shadowed with life and death, as we consider mortality, either our own, in the cases of tragic early illnesses like cancer, or that of our parents.

Of course the day we all turned forty the questions didn't change overnight, but it is true that that marker arrived in the midst of a transition for most women I know. It's interesting that even as we are aware of the weight of more complicated matters on our minds, most of us also feel liberated. We care less about the small stuff (wrinkles and linen pants, I suppose, aside).

I was one of the first of us to have babies, which means I now have some of the oldest children. As Grace nears fifteen and Whit settles into twelve, I feel the weight of their gaze on me in a new way. As soon as I got my sea legs on the storm-tossed boat of parenting, it feels like the days with my children living at home are numbered. I'm viscerally aware of wanting to be a role model for them, and that informs the things I think about and the things I do in a way that I had not anticipated in previous decades.

I know this is coming for the friends who circle me in the rapidly dimming room on Chappaquiddick. Between us we have children ranging in ages from five to fourteen, graduate degrees, full-time professional jobs, part-time professional jobs, divorces, parents who are sick or who have died. We have lived in a variety of cities across the United States. We have families of various configurations and have made a lot of different choices, but we are all the same age.

I love hearing Allison describe her forties as her favorite decade, because I feel the same way. This stage of life feels like one long exhale. It's also exhausting and overwhelming—more than any other time in my life, I feel pulled thin, and like so many people *need* me—there is no question about that. But I think most of us, at forty, find ourselves grateful for what is, even as we remain anxious about what lies ahead and sad about what will never be at the same time.

When I turned forty, two years ago, I called the decade I was entering the "thick, hot heart of life's grand pageant," and that only feels more true now. I have never loved my birthday, the same way I've never loved New Year's: I do not need to be reminded of time's drumbeat, its inexorable passage. I already feel it every day. Nevertheless, turning forty was unexpectedly thought-provoking for me, and judging by our conversations this weekend and over the past couple of years, for my friends, too.

That particular birthday ushered in a new and urgent

need to recognize and capture and appreciate my truly ordinary life. The day I turned forty, I woke up early, drove an hour and a half with my husband to pick up our children at sleepaway camp, and then came home to wash their two large trunk-loads of laundry. I went to the grocery store, we had dinner around our dining room table, and my mother surprised me by coming over for dessert. I felt like the most fortunate woman alive, and even the most mundane parts of the day felt glossed by a blossoming awareness of how holy every moment of my life is.

Since that day, my life has proceeded much the same as it had before I turned forty, replete with frustrations and exhaustion but also, now, underpinned by a sense of sturdy joy that feels new. The first couple of years of my forties were bumpy, with some medical scares and a big professional transition, but while I'm never going to be called a Zen person, I found myself, surprisingly, calmer. The changes rattled me less than they might have in the past. I don't know precisely what to ascribe that to, because in many ways the stakes seem to be going up, not down. But overall, I'm more aware of how the arc of time smooths out most bumps and am less inclined to panic about individual problems.

Every woman I know has come to her forties (those of us lucky enough to do so) with a slightly different family circumstance. Married or not, a mother or not, working or not, parents alive or ill or not living. Regardless of these differences, which can be dramatic, I'm struck by how many parts of reaching midlife feel similar. The grappling with adulthood, in all of its beauties and losses, is remarkably universal. We are all accepting that there are things that will never be, just as we look around and acknowledge what is. That acknowledgment runs the gamut from a full-on embrace to wholehearted rejection. There's also a shadow over our days of what's to come—mortality hovers around our experience now, and an awareness that the days ahead of us may not be longer than the days behind. Forty feels like we've come to the top of the Ferris wheel: the view is dazzling, in no small part because we know how quickly the descent will go.

So there's no question that turning forty is an opportunity for both reflection and inspiration, which is why I am thrilled to introduce this collection, which is brimming with both.

This book is full of reflections from individual women that also reveal and revel in the universal. From women of myriad backgrounds, a chorus rings true: the forties are a decade of reckoning and awareness, of gratitude and loss, and they are limned with emotions as divergent and powerful as the individual voices that speak to them. These women, in their forties and beyond, are in the prime of their lives.

These are not reflections on the dying of the light, but rather a full-throated celebration of what it means to be an adult woman at this moment in history.

Most of the essays in this book are written by women who are squarely a part of Generation X, and they read, also, as a powerful treatise on this generation's experience of midlife. We are exhausted, and we are happy, and we are busy, and we are trying to reckon with the costs and opportunities of the unique clarion call of our generation: that we could have it all. A promise that turns out to be both a blessing and a curse.

From musings on beauty (of course) to life post-divorce, the nostalgia of friendship, and the ever pressing question "what now?," these pieces are a dynamic and diverse kaleidoscope, but consistent themes emerge, too—a newfound clarity about what matters and what doesn't, a deepening engagement with our lives as they are, and the sorrow and elation of the truest cliché I know: time flies.

On Being
40(ish)

1

Same Life, Higher Rent

MEGHAN DAUM

Friday evening, eight p.m., early summer, New York City. I sit at my desk, face aglow in Macintosh luminescence. On the desk sits the detritus of the hour, of the day, the week, the season. There is dinner of sushi in the little takeout tray from the supermarket. There is leftover coffee in a mug from the afternoon. There are books and notebooks and checkbooks. There are pens and lip balms and hair ties and postage stamps and unmatched earrings and a Metro-Card. There are a gazillion paper napkins for some reason. There is a computer modem whose lights flash with the irregular, listing cadence of a heart murmur. There are several

Word documents up on that glowing screen, each competing for attention not so much with one another but with the email interface to which all roads lead back.

It is 1997. It is 2017. It doesn't matter. It is both. In twenty years, my life has come full circle, 360 degrees for real. People often say 360 degrees when they mean 180. They say full circle when they're really talking about a semicircle. It's an oddly human error, as though they can't quite grasp the concept of a human being turning on an axis as readily as the earth itself. But in my case it's true. At forty-seven, my life looks uncannily the same way it did at twenty-seven.

How did I get here? Nearly two decades ago, I moved from New York City to the Midwest and then to California, where I came as close to settling down as I'm probably ever going to come, which is to say I got married. Nearly two years ago, the marriage ended, and I got in the car and literally drove through my life in reverse. I drove west to east, backward in time until I landed right back where I started: alone in a scuff-marked apartment in a clanking old Manhattan building much like the one I occupied in my twenties, eating supermarket sushi at my desk and trying mightily (yes, on a Friday evening) to complete a writing assignment that was due a week ago.

There are a few differences, but they are minor. Because

it is 2017 and not 1997, I am writing on a MacBook Air laptop and not a Quadra 650. The modem is a wireless rather than a dial-up, which means that email comes in automatically and my opportunities for screen-based distraction and procrastination exceed anything I could have imagined back then. Thanks to these opportunities, I estimate that my attention span in 2017 is about 30 percent what it was in 1997. Conversely, my rent back then was 30 percent what it is now.

Same life, higher rent. This could be the motto of my life after forty-five. For many years, I had a very different life. I had what is commonly perceived of as a grown-up life, with a husband and a mortgage and a yard that required regular upkeep. There is much to be said for this life. For starters, it's a lucky thing to find someone you like enough to enlist as a partner for such an endeavor. There's also no getting around the fact that the gears of the daily grind tend to run smoother when they're greased with the benefits of coupledom. You never quite realize what a pain it is to drive yourself to every social event you attend until you have someone to share the burden with you (second glass of wine? Sure!). You never quite realize how much food you've got sitting around on high pantry shelves until there's someone who can reach it for you—and, in my case, cook it for you.

But even my 1997 self would have told you that the

membership associated with these benefits probably wasn't going to be a lifetime deal. My 1997 self would have suspected, correctly, that such benefits would lead to a severe enough case of Impostor Syndrome that I would slowly, and very sadly, wend my way back to the life I had before. What I would not have understood were the ways in which this return was less a defeat than a homecoming. I did not know that the life I was living in my twenties, a life I was certain was a temporary condition, was in fact the only one for me.

This is not to be confused with my best life or even the life I'm still on some level programmed to believe I want. I'm talking about my situational set point, the version of myself that inevitably swings back into the foreground even if I've managed to pretend to be another kind of person for a period of time. It's like an existential version of that number on the bathroom scale that manages to own you no matter what you do. You can drift above it or claw your way below it, but eventually it's always there again.

I've spent plenty of time over the years fighting my situational set point. I've lived with boyfriends and roommates and, of course, my husband. I've attempted to keep my desk neat. I've given credence to all those studies suggesting that people who live with long-term partners are healthier and live longer than sad solo dwellers who eat while standing over the sink—or in my case at my desk. I've tried to stick it out. But, always, I swing back. Like it or not, this life works for me. I love living alone. I love eating when and where and what I want. I love sleeping when I want and socializing when I want and being able to travel at the last minute without throwing another person's life out of whack as a result. I love talking to my friends on the phone for hours without worrying about someone in the next room overhearing me and (at least in my imagination) silently judging me for all the cackling gossip and bombastic complaining. I love hosting parties by myself. I love drinking that first cup of coffee in the morning while standing by my window and (did I mention I pay more rent now?) looking out at the barges floating by on the Hudson River.

All of that I did and also loved in my twenties. The only difference was that I didn't realize how much I loved it. Also, my window had a view of a brick wall.

I'll state the obvious and say that much if not all of the reason my life hasn't changed is that I'm not a parent. Children are life's great timekeepers, and when you don't live with any you're at the mercy of your own internal clock, which like everything else in the body, becomes less reliable with age. In that sense (and probably in several other senses, but who's counting?) my life is very different than that of most women in their forties, the majority of whom share their personal space with members of future generations and therefore have no trouble distinguishing the past from the present. If I had a kid, I trust I'd have no trouble either. At least I hope I wouldn't, since eating packaged sushi off a desk that's covered with hair accessories is no life for a child. Neither is having a routine in which it's possible for many days to pass in which there is no need to leave the apartment. If I felt like a recluse in my twenties, I'm a bona fide shut-in now. That's because if I need food or clothing or contact lens solution, I no longer have to go to a store to buy it. I can just click "buy now" and stay home and wait for the mail. This is a huge quality of life improvement over having to walk four blocks to CVS.

If the digital age has had a profound impact on my shopping habits, it's left my social life—at least its romantic iterations—surprisingly untouched. The dating patterns of my 1997 self and my 2017 self are virtually identical, which is to say they're sporadic, half-hearted, and marked by an attitude that lurches between grouchy and what would now be called DGAF (for the uninitiated, that's Don't Give A Fuck; a phrase I rarely use in either long or abbreviated form). In 1997, there were only two ways you could wind up on a date. You could be fixed up by a third party or you could happen to meet someone in real life, exchange phone numbers, make use of those numbers, and have an actual voice conversation in which a date is proposed and then accepted. Because of all this heavy lifting, it was rare to find yourself in a situation you might construe as a date—at least for heterosexual women in my social circles, where the underrepresentation of men in general resulted in an overrepresentation of the kind of men who couldn't be bothered to ask women out. I estimate that throughout my entire twenties, I probably had fewer than ten proper dates, by which I mean outings with men who called me on the telephone, asked me out, and bought me dinner under less-than-platonic pretenses. In retrospect, I see those men as terribly brave, not only because they had to go through all that heavy telephonic lifting but because they had to sit across the table from me, and I was just as grouchy and defeatist about the whole enterprise as I am today.

In this age of Tinder and Match.com, you can go on seven dates a week or maybe even twice that many if you have the energy without having to summon up any courage whatso-ever. At least that's what I've heard. I'll never know because every time I load a dating app onto my phone I delete it and cancel my subscription after one date. In the first two years that I was back in New York, I joined and quit OkCupid three times and went on three dates in total. The men were perfectly fine, but somehow I could never quite muster enough enthusiasm to see them again. They were interesting and smart and had twenty to thirty more years' worth of things to talk about than the men I'd dated in my twenties. But they were still no match for the solace of my apartment and the familiar rhythms of my own company. I couldn't imagine going home with any of them, partly because there's nothing I like more than going home by myself.

If that sounds like the waning desire of a middle-aged woman, I can tell you that it's not that at all. I was the same way in my twenties. The relationships I sought out back then were temporary by design, preferably long distance. I had a weakness for men whose unsuitability I could reframe as exoticism, men who didn't read books or who had troubling political beliefs or, best of all, lived far away and existed mainly as voices over the phone and occasional houseguests. I told myself I wanted a real boyfriend—and I often grew frustrated when these men inevitably stopped going through the motions of acting like one—but in hindsight I can see I wanted no such thing. I wanted the safety of impermanence. I wanted round-trip excursions on ships whose pleasures were all the sweeter for my knowing that I'd eventually be returned to my homeport.

• • •

When I got divorced, I thought I was entering act 3 of the meandering stage play of my adulthood. In this act, I thought the starting gun that I could never quite fire in my twenties would finally go off in my forties, sending me sprinting into a glorious, fully self-actualized future like some kind of nervous but nimble gazelle. I'd have the wind at my back, yet it would also be blowing gently into my face so that my hair looked amazing. I didn't turn out to be entirely wrong about this. By any objective measure, I'm doing better now than I did back then. My career is established, I'm financially solvent, and I have a slightly better wardrobe. But as good as things are, I am plagued by the feeling that whatever currency I now hold would have an exponentially higher market value if I were just ten years younger. A thirty-seven-year-old with a genuinely fulfilling and reasonably lucrative career, a decent marriage/non-catastrophic divorce under her belt, an overpriced-but-worth-it apartment, and multiple intersecting circles of friends new and old? Fantastic! The future is incandescent. The present is a sweet spot engineered for maximum forward momentum. A forty-seven-year-old with same? Meh.

I'm sure when I'm fifty-seven I'll look back on logic like that and want to smack my forty-seven-year-old self for being such an ingrate. But, for the time being, the cognitive dissonance can sometimes take my breath away. I teach in the same graduate program I myself attended more than twenty years ago. A few of my colleagues, now probably in their sixties, were professors back when I was a student. There's something wonderful about this, something that confers a sense of both achievement and coziness. Less wonderful is coming to terms with the fact that when I was a student I saw these professors as old. If you'd asked me their ages, I would have thought about it for a minute (having never specifically thought about it before) and pegged some of them for being in their sixties (which was definitely old to me at the time). I now realize they were the age I am now.

Does this mean that my students think I'm in my sixties? The notion seems preposterous, though given the way the twentysomething mind works, it also makes perfect, if devastating, sense. When you are, say, twenty-five, the adult world is a simple binary construct divided between the young and the old. The young is anyone under forty. The old is anyone over sixty. There is no in-between. The forties and fifties don't exist. The forties and fifties are just a couple of lost decades in which the only goal is to try to maintain whatever operation (child rearing, career building) you got started in your twenties and thirties. And because maintenance is so easily overlooked, so unsexy, so perennially under the radar, it is entirely possible for a twenty-five-year-old graduate student to look at her forty-seven-year-old instructor and unconsciously assume her to be a senior citizen.

This is a horrifying contemplation. Yet it's just one of a cluster of thoughts that make up the current of constant low-grade shock I feel about how old I've managed to become. At forty-seven, I could easily be a twenty-five-year-old's mother, the irony there being that if such were the case, I might actually seem even *younger* because I'd be up on pop culture and other youthful things that in my present state I don't know or care about. Most of the time, I'm relieved not to have to know or care about these things. My only exposure to contemporary popular music are the playlists inflicted on me in group fitness classes, and I can't help but think that being forced to listen to them is the sonic equivalent of being put in tortuous positions in order to tone my butt. If endless squats at a ballet barre can maintain some illusion of youth in the body, maybe blasting Kylie Minogue can do the same for the mind. I'm using Kylie Minogue as a hypothetical because the truth is, I have no idea what songs are being played in my barre class. And I'm pretty sure that given the choice between listening to Kylie Minogue and listening to a Vitamix blender, I'd choose the blender.

I'm not proud of feeling that way. In fact, it terrifies me.

Given the correlation between aging and death, declaring that you can't stand today's music might actually mark the first stage of the dying process.

And that brings me back to my apartment window, looking down at the river while listening to the same music I listened to in 1997. The big picture for me these days might be a mélange of sadness and puzzlement and oddly exhilarating resignation, but in this fleeting moment it feels nearly perfect. I have work that feeds my brain at the same time that it pays for that supermarket sushi. I have nearly a half century's worth of friends, which is something that is mathematically impossible to have in your twenties. These friends are in practically every time zone on the globe, and even when I haven't seen them in years, I can count on them to lift me up or crack me up or at the very least impart some kind of gossip that makes me think about human nature in a whole new way. I'm paying more rent than I can afford, but somehow I'm affording it anyway. The surface of my desk is as littered with paper napkins and hair accessories as it was twenty years ago, but I've met my deadlines anyway. Except for the ones I've missed.

My 1997 self would be satisfied with how things turned out, at least until I told her this was us at forty-seven and not thirty-seven.

"Is this as far as we got?" she might ask.

"Ask me in ten years," I might answer.

Except I already know the answer. It's as far as we got. It's as far as we were ever supposed to get. I may not always live in this apartment or even in this city. I may not always live by myself. I may grow tired of the sushi. But on some cellular level it will always be Friday evening, eight p.m., alone at a messy desk. No matter what I do, my situational pendulum will swing back to this place. As anticlimactic as that is, it's also just as it should be. Everything has its set point. Except the rent, of course. The rent always goes up.

2

Soul Mates: A Timeline in Clothing

CATHERINE NEWMAN

1972

I am wearing bell-bottomed jeans and a hand-me-down down jacket with a fake-fur-trimmed snorkel hood. She is wearing red-and-white-checked pants and a plush red coat that I covet. We are four years old and holding hands at the bus stop after school. We are in Mrs. Saffer's kindergarten class, we collect Wacky Packs, we take swim lessons at the YMCA, and we have older brothers who are, like us, best friends. I would know these facts anyway, but they also happen to be written in Mrs. Saffer's handwriting under a drawing in my scrapbook titled "My Friend."

1975

We are both wearing pink lipstick and fringed head scarves with shower-ring hoop earrings sewn to them. It's New York City, so in one efficient trip through somebody's high rise, you can fill a pillowcase with Bit-O-Honey and Whistle Pops and candy cigarettes. "Trick or treat!" we say and, sometimes, in answer to the inevitable question, "Gypsies!"

1978

We are wearing egg on our faces—or just the whites, as per the pore-tightening mask recipe in her sister's *Seventeen* magazine, despite our unblemishedness. Also we are wearing save-the-whales buttons and striped Pro-Keds sneakers and enormous cake- and soda-flavored Bonne Bell Lip Smackers that dangle around our necks from ropes. The Beatles' Red Album spins on her parents' turntable, and we lie on our backs on the shaggy white carpet singing lyrics I don't understand. Norwegian Wood (what?) and Eleanor Rigby, whom I confuse with Eleanor Roosevelt. ("Why did she keep her face in a jar by the door?" I ask my parents once while we're watching a PBS special on first ladies, and they, understandably, don't know what I'm asking.) Coolly, she can't decide between John and George. Lamely, I like Paul.

1980

I wear rainbow suspenders and knee pads and quad skates with sparkly red wheels. I wear pigtails and bangs and a gappy smile where two of my grown-up teeth refuse to show up and grow in. I wear my own chest like a vest knit from flatness itself, and I read and reread a picture book called *Leo the Late Bloomer*. She wears her long, dark hair parted in the middle. She reads *To Kill a Mockingbird*, and beneath her dark sweater, something is blooming.

1981

To the many bar mitzvahs we attend, we wear khaki-green baby-wale corduroy knickers and white, lace-trimmed Gunne Sax blouses and Kork-Ease sandals (hers with suntan stockings; mine with, sigh, white knee-high socks). In our everyday life, like now, lying in her top bunk with a swiped copy of *Our Bodies, Ourselves*, we wear braces and $M\star A\star S\star H$ T-shirts. I wear ceramic star-shaped pins and dangly braided-ribbon barrettes. We wear an iridescent shade of lip gloss called Blue Rose. She wears ooh-la-la Sasoon jeans, but I'm not allowed, so I wear just plain Levi's. "Did you do this?" Her handsome brother is standing in the doorway in a blue-and-white-striped alligator shirt and a smudgy mustache, coolly furious and holding a tape recorder. He presses play, and we hear him warble briefly in cracking Hebrew before it cuts out and we hear her singing "Maybe" from *Annie*, very vibrato. "Did you record yourself singing over my Haftora practice tape?" he says, and she says, "No."

1983

We are wearing zip-ankled jeans, maybe? Benetton sweaters, perhaps? Whatever it is, it is covered in barf. We have snuck a bottle of vodka from her parents' dinner party and drunk it. She walks me the five blocks home, both of us reeling, and when I ask her later how she got back to her own house, she has no idea. We tell our parents we have stomach viruses— the kind of virus, I suppose, that makes you vomit up giant, clear pools of vodka—and they pretend to believe us.

1986

We wear R.E.M. T-shirts and vintage rhinestone jewelry and Madonna-style bandannas in our hair. We wear Anaïs Anaïs eau de toilette and kohl eyeliner that we draw practically right onto our eyeballs. We wear our dads' old suit jackets with the sleeves rolled up. We wear hickeys and rug burns and contraceptive sponges, and we walk each other home, swapping stories about boyfriends and sex. We wear our own taut and gorgeous skin like a bespoke suit made from nectarines.

1989

In the photograph, she's wearing Ray-Bans, a black miniskirt, a Yale sweatshirt, and a dark bob that frames her Italian-movie-star face. She's holding out a cut-open blood orange to show the camera its garnet flesh, and the great domed cathedral looms behind her. Every photograph from our semester abroad is like this, like a caricature of Italy: the frescoes and the Chianti and the risotto and the Vespas, and always the Duomo, peeking over everyone's shoulder like a photobomber. We kind of have the time of our lives, and also it is kind of terrible. We wear underwear that we wash out in the bidet, and we are occasionally homesick and often confused, catcalled practically to death. When we get home, we each wear new leather lace-up shoes and an extra twenty pounds, like a flesh souvenir.

1990

In two different states, we wear caps and gowns. She stays east and I move west, and we wear 501s and, beneath our political T-shirts (Silence = Death), lacy black bras. I am also wearing a bike helmet most of the time because I haven't learned how to drive yet. She rides the subway and will never learn how to drive.

1994

She is in New York, wearing Doc Martens and slippy little Betsey Johnson dresses. I am in California, wearing off-brand combat boots and slippy little thrift-store dresses. "I don't know," she writes in a letter, "if I'm doing what I want to be doing." I don't know either.

1996

I am still in Santa Cruz. I wear silver flip-flops and cutoff overalls over lacy little girls'-department undershirts. She is still in New York. She wears tall leather boots and Clinique lipstick that matches her dark cashmere sweaters. We both wear glasses and pearl earrings. My boyfriend and I are in grad school, and every night is baked-potato night; she is making documentary films, dating a finance guy, and eating out in SoHo. We wish we had each other's life; we wish we had the same life as each other.

1999

In her handsome brother's wedding pictures, she is draped in something dark and lacy and I have my arm slung around her, wearing an eggplant-colored empire-waist dress with a giant baby growing beneath it. I hold this picture out to my husband now and say, "I look like a teen-pregnancy after-school special," and he agrees. We felt so grown-up that we'd lost track of how young we were.

2001

I am back east for good, wearing black leggings, black Dansko clogs, big silver hoop earrings, and a Stevie Nicks kind of flowy green dress. She is wearing white satin Mary Janes and a white floor-length spaghetti-strap gown. All fifty of the buttons running up the back have fallen off—they were tacked on by the tailor, it turns out, not stitched properly—and I sew them on, trying not to poke her with the needle while she stands in front of me, crying and cracking up. Later, during my toast, I joke that I'm the one she should be marrying. Luckily, everybody laughs.

2003

She is wearing my old black maternity tunic, stretched over what will be her firstborn. I am wearing a child on my hip, a beige nursing bra with three-inch-wide straps, and a backpack containing an enormous baby in a striped onesie. "Seriously?" she says, pointing to my leaky fun-house breasts, and I say, "Just you wait."

2005

She is not wearing the scarf I knit her, because I have never finished it. "Does anyone ever actually finish knitting a scarf?" she wonders. We're wearing flannel pajamas, drinking red wine out of jelly jars, eating organic Cheetos from a crinkly bag, and whispering because a pile of babies is asleep in the next room. If we decided to run away from home, we could pack in the bags under our eyes. "We should make a fake documentary called *The Unfinished Scarf Project*," she muses. "Someone gathers up all the half-knit scarves . . ." She's an actual filmmaker, but this is pretty much as far as any idea gets right now. We should make a documentary called *The Unfinished Conversation Project*. It would just be us talking in abstracted bursts while the babies cry and tug on their footie pajamas and choke on grapes.

2007

We wear worn-thin patience and fake smiles because we are sharing a hotel room and the baby is crying and all the kids are awake and unhappy and we have lots of ideas about who should be doing what differently. Years later, I will regret this. We are wearing white terry-cloth hotel bathrobes, our hair piled up, because we are about to sneak out to the hot tub with a thermos full of wine and the baby monitor where everything will be okay again beneath the stars.

2011

At the beach in Maine, the kids are wearing sand and sea-water and streaks of Popsicle. She is wearing her own hair, her healthy body, and, like me, a regular, baggy Lands' End tankini that needs only to conceal her regular, baggy mom belly rather than, say, an ileostomy bag, a chemo port, and the scarred cartography of a dozen surgeries, none of which she has. We don't even think to marvel at this fact.

2013

They won't call this a remission, but her hair is growing back in now, a silvering accidental pixie that she wears with a blue-and-white-striped boatneck and little cropped jeans. "You look like Jean Seberg in *Breathless*," I say. I can't take my eyes off her. She's so tiny I should just pop her into my pocket for safekeeping. She has started a popcorn business, and the house smells like butter and brown sugar, bourbon and vanilla and the corn itself. I'm wearing my awkward good health like it's a hulking giant, fee-fi-fo-fumming around her kitchen in a white apron.

2015 (February)

I am wearing the same gray sweatshirt dress I've been wearing for three days. She is wearing white thigh-high medical compression stockings, a poly-blend johnny, and a PICC line. Also, because she is freezing to death, a chunky purple wool shawl and a waffle-weave cotton blanket from the warmer. We are lying together in her hospice bed, wearing our grief like a python around our ribs, like a plastic bag over our faces, like the black dress I'll be wearing a week from now. She is wearing blue fingernail polish that I ran out to buy at the Coney Island Rite Aid after she was craving watermelon, then chocolate, then glamour. When I hold them in mine to paint their tips, her fingers feel like bones. I am wearing my winter boots because the ice machine is down the hall, and there is a lot of ice that is required, and I feel strange padding through the quiet hospice in only my wool socks. We watch the clouds skid over the Atlantic, watch a curtain of sleet and then the sun itself sink into the ocean. "Kidnap me," she says, and I say, "Where should we go?" "Anywhere," she says, and falls asleep. The impossibly young music therapist tiptoes in, sings "Across the Universe," strumming her guitar like an angel.

2015 (June)

"It's like the best thrift store ever," I say. "Everything's free and nice and your size. But it all makes you cry." Her sister and niece and sister-in-law and stepdaughter and I are in her closet in our underpants, zipping into corduroys and summer skirts, pulling on tank tops and cotton sweaters, the clothes as familiar to me as my own, except it all smells exactly like her. I set aside a few things for her boys: a Beatles tee; her Yale sweatshirt; all the good jewelry. Her wedding dress is zippered inside a long plastic bag and I can't look at it—I push her red winter coat up against it so I don't have to see it. "I don't actually want anything," the others say, one at a time, weirding themselves out about a dead person's clothing. But I do. I want everything.

Now I am wearing her striped Boden tunics to work; I am wearing her ancient Norma Kamali nightshirt to bed; I am wearing her expensive yoga pants and the Ugg boots I coveted (ugh) and the dangly-heart earrings I made her when she turned eleven. "Are you sure you're happy, wearing all her clothes?" a friend asks, and I am, although happy is not the right word. I am wearing my heart on my sleeve, my memories like a crazy quilt of loss. My funny, sweet-hearted teenager offers to make me a silk screen: "My best friend died of ovarian cancer, and all I got was this lousy T-shirt."

Oh, but more. I got so much more.

3

It's a Game of Two Halves

VERONICA CHAMBERS

I was never the cool type of girl who knows a lot about sports. But along the way I've picked up a few things. I grew up in Brooklyn, where I spent decades rooting for the Knicks. And every once in a while, I was offered that holy grail of tickets: Madison Square Garden, near courtside, where the celeb watching was as good as anywhere in Hollywood. I also had season tickets for the WNBA for three summers and that was girl-power awesome. Then I married a football fan, and the gridiron entered my life. Truthfully, I still don't fully understand football. Yet, some of my best memories involve hazy Sunday afternoons when my daughter was a baby and my husband would sit on the couch, a beer in one hand, the baby in the other, their faces lit up by the TV screen. My daughter would tip her bottle to the side in an almost comic mirror image of my husband's beer and sit, enraptured, watching the game.

These days the sport we all get riled up about is soccer, especially during the World Cup. During the last World Cup, I scheduled every single lunch meeting at a Latin restaurant that had installed giant TVs for the purpose. I love how whenever I watch the World Cup it feels like my heart has been gifted one of those round-the-world tickets. With each game, I get on and off virtual planes. Here I am in England, rooting for the Brits. Now I'm in Cameroon, cheering for the red, gold, and green. France versus Spain is always a tug-of-war. I love both countries, even while recognizing their weaknesses. Watching soccer is fun, it's easy to follow, and it's a small investment of a few weeks with this intense, exhilarating payoff.

What I have learned from being a sort-of sports fan is a lesson that I have applied, really almost daily, to the act and art of being in my forties: it's a game of two halves. And this is the thing: no matter what happens, you can't win in the first half. Victory is only decided in the very last seconds of the second half. So when I turned forty, I did the most unusual thing for myself: I decided to take it easy. I decided that I was going to take the first half of my forties a little easier: take the time to stretch my legs, score a goal or two if I could, but mostly I wanted to take some time to think about what mattered to me. What did winning mean to me on the most personal of levels, and what would it take to get there?

This was, to put it mildly, out of character. Ever since I heard the word "wunderkind"—most likely on a cartoon of some sort—I've wanted to be one. I was never a real prodigy at anything, but I pushed toward success as hard and as fast as I could. I went to college at sixteen. Cowrote my first book at twenty-one. Became an editor at the *New York Times Magazine* at twenty-three. When I look back on my twenties, it's like a music video for the remix of Donna Summer's "She Works Hard for the Money" and Rihanna's "Work." It was really just work, work, work. (And more work, work, work.)

In retrospect, this wasn't a bad thing. When I got my first big book deal, I used part of my advance to take a photography trip to Morocco. I thought (naively) that I would meet a guy: a globe-trotting, twentysomething *National Geographic* photographer kind of guy, and that we would fall madly in love. Then I arrived in Morocco and realized that most twentysomethings don't take two-week vacation courses: too expensive, too many days off burned up in one go. The trip was filled with older people—not my parents' age, my *grandparents'* age. Almost everyone was retired. I wasn't that disappointed. I was in Morocco. I took thousands of photos, and I had all of these grandparent types fawning over me. One guy, named Edward, had sold his family's small department store brand to a big conglomerate. He watched me working throughout our trip: faxing back my assignments (those were the days of faxes!) at every hotel. He observed my datelessness. And he explained that he had worked nonstop in his twenties. "You can have your fun now or you can have your fun later," he explained. "But if you're lucky, you can work hard when you're young, which can be kind of fun. Then you have more time and resources later to kick back."

I understood what he meant. Yes, I was completely nerding out in my twenties. But I was a magazine editor who covered pop culture. I didn't have much of a life outside of work, but my work involved traveling to movie sets, attending music festivals and the occasional boondoggle: like the time I spent three days in Villa d'Este in Lake Como with Ricky Martin and two dozen Asian music journalists, one of whom became one of my very best friends. I was working, but it was a helluva lot of fun.

Like many women, my thirties signified a shift: marriage, motherhood. These brought with them a feeling of security and lots of good times. But when I look back on that decade, the image that comes up most readily is the constant hum of bleary-eyed exhaustion: it's two a.m. and there are work deadlines and a baby to feed and aging relatives in the hospital. When I think of my thirties, what I think of most often is looking over at my husband and giving him that "Are we having fun yet?" smile. Happy to be together. No idea how we are going to get from one day to the next.

Which is all to say I wanted my forties—the start of the second half of life so to speak—to be more deliberate. I flung myself through my twenties: defying sleep and a social life to work my butt off. My thirties was like one long military crawl: I slogged through marriage and motherhood, family obligations and multiple moves. So often, it felt like the goal was just to survive, to get from point A to B. I wanted my forties to be different. I cast about for role models over forty. I aspired to be Emma Thompson smart and funny and, if I could manage it, Cate Blanchett well dressed and hot, in that icy, not-trying kind of way. Mostly, though, I wanted to be happy: I wanted to become less goal oriented and to somehow sculpt my days so that I could do more of the things that I loved and less of the things that I hated.

On the eve of my fortieth birthday, I made a list of ten things that would define, for me, winning the decade. It was less of a checklist and more of a blueprint for the shape of my life: where I wanted to live, how much money I hoped to save and how much I hoped to give away, what kind of work I wanted to be doing, traditions I hoped to forge with my daughter, ways in which I wanted to deepen my marriage with my husband. The list symbolized for me how I wanted to *be* in the world vs. the goals and resolutions of previous decades, which were focused on what I wanted to *do*. In honor of that ageless beauty, Janet Jackson, I called it my "design of a decade."

Every year, I check in on the list. One item on the list, I hit right away. There are three items that I hit every year, more or less if I'm being generous to myself, which I aspire to be. I'm smack-dab in the middle of my forties, and there are six items still floating around in the ether. Oddly enough, I don't feel super rushed about them. I will either hit them by fifty or they will become the foundation of the design of my next decade. After being someone who skipped grades and skipped ladders in the career rung earlier in my life, I am now, at forty-five, finally becoming someone who knows how to slow down. Ten big-picture aspirations that make my heart sing and the luxurious timeline of ten years to accomplish them feels very much like a gift I've given myself.

I'm not as old, or nearly as wealthy, as my department

store magnate friend that I met in Morocco. But I have had, in my forties, the kind of fun that my twentysomething-year-old self could never have imagined. I spent my forty-second birthday in Paris, and although it's a city that, over the years, I've spent a lot of time in, I will never forget doing the most touristy of things that year: climbing to the top of the Eiffel Tower with my then five-year-old daughter and the smiles on both of our faces when we got to the top. One fall, my husband and I rented a friend's country house for three months and spent every weekend in the woods. My heart leaps when I think of how many dinners we had with our friends at that house: on the screened-in porch during the mild days, by the wood-burning stove on the cold days. This past week, in the middle of moving cross-country, we hosted two dinner parties. One was a rollicking red beans and rice dinner party for twenty-four, with a guest chef, an amazing man from New Orleans named Pableaux Johnson who was named one of the one hundred best home cooks in America. Then the night before the move, we had a pool party with some of our closest family friends. The kids were in the pool until ten p.m. The adults were laughing and telling stories until nearly midnight. My husband, daughter, and I actually missed our flight the next day, that's how far behind we were. Yet, it was all such a magnificent win.

At twenty-five, I had no boyfriend. My best (girl)friend had dumped me. I spent that Christmas alone in my apartment sobbing my eyes out. If my life were a movie, a thirteen-going-on-thirty-style comedy, my twenty-five-year-old self would look at my forty-five-year-old self and say, "Wait? What? You lived in Paris? You have a cute husband and an adorable daughter? You have dinner parties—like, all the time? It all worked out? You're not eating Lean Cuisine over the sink after a too-long day at work and falling asleep on the couch? And wait, let me look in your closet. Who bought you that Chanel dress and that Edie Parker purse that says 'Baller'? *You* bought them with your own money? Wow, wait. You *are* a baller."

I don't give myself credit for it nearly enough, but I know the younger me would be proud of the woman I've become.

This idea, of the woman I wanted to become, is ever more powerful to me. One of the items on my list is that I really want to be trilingual. I know, insert eye roll. But languages have long been one of my passions. My family is from Panama. I grew up with my mom speaking Spanish to my brother and me, but we answered in English. It was like this impossible divide that I couldn't cross: understanding Spanish but not being able to speak it. Then when I started junior high school, I opted to take Spanish instead of what was mandated: French. At the end of a year, I could speak to my mother. In two years, I could read and write and converse with my whole extended family. By the time I got to college, I was reading novels in Spanish and very occasionally, dreaming in Spanish.

I went on to study Russian for four years in college, then in my late twenties, I studied Japanese and spent a good amount of time in Japan. I started traveling to Paris and spent a year in France, where I picked up just enough French to get around, order in restaurants, and do my weekly market shopping. In that blender of language, my grip on Spanish loosened. I could always speak to people when I traveled, and I could speak to my mom, but I lost the ability to read novels. So a few years ago I started taking a Spanish film and conversation class. Once a week, I would watch the assigned film, and then on a Tuesday night, I'd go to the class where a teacher would guide us through conversation about the film. It was so much fun to realize after watching an astronaut movie that there was a whole world of vocabulary that I'd never used before. It reminded me, in an odd way, of Elizabeth Alexander's beautiful poem "The Venus Hottentot": "Elegant facts await me. / Small things in the world are mine."

•   •   •

While I devote an inordinate amount of my time thinking about how to game my metabolism and get Helen Mirren hot, I also spend a good deal of time thinking about what it means to be wise. One of the questions I have been asking myself, here in my forties, is what is wisdom? What can I trust with a deep knowing that doesn't require validation or a Facebook hive mind poll or running it by a friend? One of the things that seems extraordinarily clear to me is that if we are lucky, time passes and we get older. We cannot control it all: especially the shocks and surprises, the heartbreak, the unexpected deaths of those we love and those we barely know but think of fondly. But we are free to imagine what the future will look like, and we would, I think, be wise to think of how much of that future it is in our power to shape. When I'm talking to my daughter, or to my friends, I want to own the experience of having two decades of adult life under my belt. My mother's generation may have had their issues, but they weren't afraid of being adults. In contrast, I think sometimes when I'm looking at a group of fortysomething women who could pass for thirty, and we're all saying, "Who's the grown-up here?" that we owe it to each other, to our families, to our daughters, to ourselves, to spend at least as much time on our interior life as we do on trying to look cute in our jeans. So I meditate. I read spiritual books (I'm a big Marianne Williamson/*A Course in Miracles* girl), and I go, usually once a year, to some sort of mind-body retreat.

One way that I've sought to gather wisdom in my forties is by attending a weekend retreat with the great Buddhist writer Pema Chödrön. This is something I've done twice and that I aspire to do at least once more. Pema talks about the idea of "good in the beginning, good in the middle, and good at the end." It's a way of breaking down any practice to be mindful and focused with good intentions, be it the act of eating a simple meal or working on a project with a colleague or saying goodbye to someone who is terminally ill. You make mistakes. You hit walls. You lose your way, but you keep coming back to the practice with an open heart. You try to make it good in the beginning. Maybe that doesn't work. So you try again. Good in the middle is another chance. But maybe you lose your patience or your temper, and you blow it. Then try for good at the end; try to end what you are doing with as much grace and generosity and warmth as you can manage—toward yourself and toward others.

I think that "good in the beginning, good in the middle, good at the end" is a kind of a Buddhist take on a game of two halves. It's become a way for me to break everything down into a chance for me to do better. This month has been chockablock with work. But as I move toward the fifteenth, I urge myself to relax. I take out my calendar and schedule all of my meetings and appointments for the last two weeks of the month for after three p.m. I've still got to work. I've still got a ton to do. But maybe in the mornings, I can breathe and move a little more slowly.

Every season seems to me a game of two halves. If fall brings that back-to-school rush and the return-from-summer-vacation sprint back to work, then I try to look at late October, early November, that time right before Thanksgiving and the holidays, as a chance to rethink and reset. What do I need more of? What do I want less of? Winter, spring, and especially summer seem so easy to break into two parts: one half to just live through, the other half to experiment with, fine-tune what's working, tweak what's not.

Even a twenty-four-hour period offers the chance for recovery and a redo. When three p.m. comes and the day has been a nonstop shit storm, I think, how can I eke out a little bit of a win here? A drink with a friend. A dinner that I know I'll love. Even just a shower and in bed by eight, the same bedtime as my daughter, can feel like a treat.

I don't know a single woman who feels like she's got it all perfectly sussed and sorted. By forty, I think we all have a plus and minus column. The things that make us proud and the things that make us cringe. But this is the thing. We made it. Getting to forty without dying is like getting into a giant nightclub after spending a very, very long time in line and besting the most mercurial of bouncers: the universe. You're in now. The music is blaring. There are plenty of options for beverages (including mocktails if you've discovered that you really shouldn't drink alcohol). You're wearing something cute and shoes that you can dance in. You're in this club and there are a whole lot of girls who couldn't get in no matter how badly they wanted to. Lena Dunham can't come. Natalie Portman is amazing, but she can't get in—not yet. Zoë Kravitz may be an old soul but the bouncer at the front won't take her fake ID. This is a fortysomething club and you are partying with the likes of Octavia Spencer and Amy Poehler, Tracee Ellis Ross and Cameron Diaz. Look around! There's Melissa McCarthy, Zadie Smith, Lucy Liu, Sofia Coppola, and Toni Collette. Our sixty-, seventy-, and eightysomething mentors: Oprah, Meryl Streep, Rita Moreno, and Helen Mirren are up in the VIP booth dropping science like the boss babes that they are. The DJ—I nominate Sandra Cisneros—is manning the wheels of steel.

Yes, I have these goals and aspirations, some of them, like the whole "I want to be a French girl, damn it," can seem quite twee. But one of the gifts of this age is knowing how good it feels when I treat my life like a party I really, really want to be at. This decade is a dance floor. In the very best moments, there are no mirrors on the wall, just the smiling faces of the people I love looking back at me. Which is why, as much as humanly possible, both literally and figuratively, I get out there and I bust a move.

The biggest
surprise of
life after
forty is . . .

"Is that it wasn't that different than thirty-nine, except it sounded so much more different. With ages, it's so much how it sounds, not how it feels."

—Julie Klam

"The biggest surprise about turning forty was that so little about my life was anything—and I mean, anything—like I would've predicted even five years before. That, and the fact that I finally felt ready to step away from struggling with my life and live it instead."

—Jena Schwartz

"New friends. I'd assumed that by forty we pretty much have all the friends we'll ever get. But over the last several years I've embarked on first-rate friendships that have shown me friend-making never stops, unless we want it to."

—Kate Bolick

"Finding the courage of my convictions. I don't know everything but I know what I believe in and what I'm willing to fight for."

—Veronica Chambers

"How much my vagina sweats at night."

—Catherine Newman

4

What We Talk about When We Talk about Our Face

SLOANE CROSLEY

*L*ike everyone living on the planet, I would rather not die the kind of death that requires an autopsy. Unlike everyone living on the planet, I have a detailed list of reasons why. While an aversion to being murdered ranks high, there are also, shall we say, more minor indignities. On any given day, my skin is carrying trace amounts of so many beauty products, my toxicology report would read as if Ken Starr wrote it. And I'm old enough to have lived that reference. Back when I was a teenager, products were toys. I gravitated toward body lotions that smelled nice and masks that cracked when I smiled. But now, in the swan song of my thirties, I have a medicine cabinet brimming with eye gels, face mists, exfoliating scrubs, night creams, day creams, midafternoon creams, every-other-Tuesday creams. Come winter, I use a rose petal serum once foisted on me by an impassioned homeopath. I mix it into foot lotion. I *own* foot lotion. Given how much time I spend applying these various concoctions, it's a wonder I'm not still typing this from the bathroom.

Do you now suspect you're in for a polemic about collagen masks? Well, I don't blame you, but you can relax (and should, because brow-furrowing causes wrinkles). This is about beauty, sure, but beauty as it pertains to youth. Youth is a rich and venerable subject. It's the basis for half the novels, operas, and art ever produced (sex would account for the other half). The only snag is, if you're a woman living in our media-saturated century, what you are regularly digesting is no longer a conversation about youth—it's a conversation about beauty. One used to be the fraternal twin of the other. For centuries, women wanted to be perceived as beautiful because it was a sign of fertility, an advertisement for the hospitality of their wombs. Beauty was mostly an indicator of health, of being strong enough to weather long winters on the farm—or wealth, of being rich enough to get your teeth fixed. But beauty as we know it has become a separate jurisdiction. It has been cleaved from youth, and as a result women are encouraged to achieve something that has little significance beyond an aesthetic one.

In theory, this is an empowering idea—beauty for beauty's sake, not just biologically suitability. But in practice? Beauty has morphed into yet another category of concern that women must either embrace or, at minimum, wrestle with. Ask yourself: Would you rather be five years younger but much less attractive than you are now or five years older but much more attractive than you are now? If you even had to *think* about it, welcome. You're in the correct century.

This is why I, personally, tend to avoid conversations about maintaining one's looks. Despite my well-stocked bathroom, the subject always feels foreign to me. As a reader, I find beauty articles intimidating. No matter the artistry of their execution or the veracity of their science, they make me feel underqualified to be female. As if I've latched on to news of a distant civil war six years into it. *New technology when it comes to oxygen masks!* I didn't know there was old technology. And as a writer, I am skeptical about chucking myself into bathtubs of viscous goop or getting piranha pedicures for the sake of journalism. Don't get me wrong—I enjoy receiving a free facial as much as the next gal. But would I pay a technician to laser beam my pores with my own money? Absolutely not.

I have no desire to shame women who choose to pour more time and money into their beauty routines than I do. And I'm not exempt from extremes—I am a complete crazy person when it comes to my hair. Like a real lunatic. The thing I find hard to swallow is the pretense that any of these treatments or products will cauterize the wounds of time. That any of them will prevent age or distract me from the realities of mortality. That any of them will, as the creams promise, "activate youth." At the time of my writing this, I am thirty-eight years old (which, because of our cultural tick of waiting twelve months before we start counting, means I'm actually in my thirty-ninth year). Time will tell if I need any of my skin-care routines. And by the time it does it will, ironically, be too late.

An assessment of my face as it stands now: Construction projects that began in my late twenties are still under way. Wrinkles are being dug like trenches into my forehead, nose pores expanded, under-eye skin rolled thin, lip hairs freshly arrived and ready to party. On the bright side, the chipmunk cheeks that caused me such woe as a child are paying off as an adult. I may no longer look twenty-eight, but I do, paradoxically, sometimes look twelve. If packing for a trip in a hurry, I feel confident going anywhere in the world with only face lotion, toothpaste, and deodorant. Like Ally Sheedy's character in *The Breakfast Club*, "I can run away, and I can go to the ocean, I can go to the country, I can go to the mountains. I could go to Israel, Africa, Afghanistan." But this begs the question: Why do I slather all this junk on at home if I don't actually need it?

It's not because it can't hurt. A little thingy of under-eye gel is seventy dollars. Believe me, it can hurt. It's that in recent years, I have found there is something lurking beneath the surface aside from loosening muscle tissue. I have been in deep-beauty denial. Because I have found discussions about appearance to be one hollow endeavor ladled atop another, I have not taken the time to understand what it is I'm truly after when I hose myself down with hydrating sprays. Half the time I think I'm doing it because I'm a sucker for packaging. But it's not the packaging. And it's not prettiness I'm after, exactly. Or allure. Nor is it time travel—I'm not delusional. No, two years shy of forty and I find that what I really want more than anything is to pause my face. Not to rewind it, but to freeze time like Evie in *Out of This World*—a show about a half-alien teenage girl that no one born after 1985 has heard of.

Call it magical thinking, but I genuinely believe that unless I have made enough proactive decisions about my life, my face is not allowed to follow suit. It's just not. It is not allowed to look more or less beautiful on the surface until I answer some deeper questions about my existence. Have I created enough, loved enough, been loved enough, accomplished enough, and learned enough to have earned these burgeoning forehead wrinkles? Is my life rooted in other people in such a way that I don't feel the need to cover up my own roots, cutting off the crown of my head in Instagram photos? Am I comfortable in my own skin, recognizing it as immutable packaging despite whatever negligible improvements products can provide? In short: Do I have enough behind me to face what's in front of me?

When I look at my thirty-eight-year-old face in the mirror, I generally don't think much beyond "Yup, there goes my face." But when I do reflect on my reflection, this is where my mind lands—on the desire to press pause and take stock. *Hold up, Under-Eye Bags, I need to assess my whole life before you settle in.*

On the bright side, at this age I no longer wish for a specific checklist of physical traits as I did in my twenties and early thirties. I think about the years I spent self-conscious that I had a chin like Jay Leno and I cringe. Or how I wanted a smaller butt or tanner legs or eyes that didn't sink into my face when I smiled. Or the moments I let living in a city filled *to the brim* with supermodels get me down. It's not that I have reached some divinely humble state in which I don't care how I look. Or how they look. It's that what I care about more than anything else is having my insides align with my outsides. Not the other way around.

You might think that all milestone birthdays invite this intense level of stocktaking, especially for women. But I assure you that thirty-year-olds (at least this former thirty-year-old) don't think like this. I have proof. Nine years ago, I wrote an essay for British *Elle* about my anticipation around turning thirty. Rather, their anticipation. The magazine assumed I would have reflections in the bank, ruminations ready to go. I had none. This did not prevent me from taking the assignment.

In the essay, I confessed that part of my ambivalence about aging stemmed from the fact that I had been pro-actively ignoring articles like the one I was writing—what could age you more than thinking so hard about age? And let's face it: the only report younger women want from the future is that it holds more happiness and continued hotness. I didn't think the readers of British *Elle* wanted to hear about how getting older can be full of harsh realities such as a zero-tolerance hangover policy and sporadic knee pain. This hunch was more or less confirmed by the accompanying image the magazine ran, that of a laughing model who looked to be in college, wearing a dress made of safety pins.

I also confessed a strange idea I held. I didn't worry so much about thirty because I assumed I was going to wake up the day of and find myself magically transformed into an adult. I anticipated thirty as "a kind of shutdown of my former self." Ten years later and no part of me, not even the most secret part, thinks in such Kafkaesque terms. For one thing, if it were possible to jettison one's current self, why would one have to wait for a birthday to do it? For another, the bonus decade of life experience has taught me that I am stuck with me. The name of the game now is to work with that, not to become someone else. It's like Confucius said: "No matter where you go, there you are." And that guy had a very wrinkly forehead.

As I reread the *Elle* essay before sitting down to write this one, I forgave twenty-nine-year-old me for her various misconceptions. She was barely an adult, what did she know? Let's just let her off with a warning. Until I got to the final paragraph. Wanting to cover my bases with older readers who would surely want to reach through the page and slap a twenty-nine-year-old (quoth *Sex and the City*: "Twenty-five! Fuck, I'm old!"), I wrote that fretting about turning thirty "will probably sound ridiculous to me when I'm fifty."

I had skipped a decade. And I'm absolutely sure I did it on purpose.

Was I afraid of offending forty-year-olds by putting them at the tail end of the spectrum? Why not just solve the problem by pushing it to eighty? I think it's because, at twenty-nine, I felt I had a better grasp on eighty than I did on forty. Eighty is undeniably old. This is not tactlessness, it's biology. But forty is right on the edge between old and young, an age where visual cues, financial brackets, and biological age could make one forty-year-old seem thirty and the next seem fifty. It's a difficult age to make snap generalizations about. Everyone's forty is different. Even how one feels at forty depends on what I like to call Internal Age Vision. For example, my IAV is 32/68—meaning that most days I walk around feeling thirty-two with sharp spikes of sixty-eight. But I have some peers who are 48/85 (best not to call after ten p.m.) and others who are 24/19 (best not to call before noon).

The other day, I told a concerned twenty-six-year-old not to worry so much about being in the right career, that she has plenty of time to make mistakes. This is not hugely original advice, but it does happen to be true. I can't *fathom* telling a forty-year-old the same thing. The stakes are so much higher up here. Is this hypothetical forty-year-old worried about changing careers? About getting tenure? About marrying the wrong partner? About never finding the right one? About the health of her children? About not being as successful as she once was? You know what? Maybe she should be worried. Four decades on Earth is long enough to know what constitutes a stressful situation.

To further complicate matters, our forty is vastly different from our parents' forty. My life as it stands now (in a relationship but not married, renting but not owning, sitting on a $600 chair but typing at a desk I screwed together in 1999) barely resembles my early exposure to the age. Born of baby boomers, who had children younger, I am a member of the last generation that will remember their parents at forty. I mean truly remember them. My father played competitive tennis when he was younger, and I have clear recollections of getting beaten by him on a regular basis. (Which probably says as much about his age as it does about mine, as the alleged problem with millennials is that they were raised by people who let them win.) For his fortieth birthday, my mother threw him a surprise party in our house. She wore a gold lame blouse with shoulder pads, and she emerged from the kitchen with a cake designed to look like a tennis court, complete with plastic players. I remember the party. I remember guests crowding around the cake. I remember taking two sips of champagne and acting drunk, thinking this would cause the more suffocating factions of my parents' friends to leave me alone. Little did I know adults are perversely amused by the idea of a drunk child.

Now the idea of having a whole person around, hewn of my genetic material and recording my sartorial choices, is unthinkable. I am comfortable with the idea of birthing babies of my own and, thanks to my girlfriends, am already an expert in giraffe-shaped teething toys. But my sister was sixteen and I was ten years old by the time my parents were my age. A ten-year-old can read novels. A ten-year-old can judge you, keep a cell phone, and set the house on fire. And most importantly, I don't *look* old enough to have given birth to a ten-year-old . . . do I?

At least I'm not alone in all this. My Comrades of the Fourth Decade are equally conflicted about their facades. They, too, admit that their makeup-free days might be drawing to a close. They, too, want a moment to pause and assess. They are not insecure or vain, though we are all sometimes those things—they are just trying to read the tea leaves of their own faces, to give beauty the meaning it's lost in order to better understand themselves. How can anyone blame us when we're getting zits between our wrinkles?

Last week, in an effort to make a thirty-nine-year-old

friend feel better about her impending birthday, I told her forty would be the start of a new decade. The chance to shake things up! Why, she is one of God's little Etch A Sketches. Let us rejoice!

This did not go over well, especially coming from someone younger, even if by a lousy couple of years.

"Look at these!" she cried, lifting her bangs and leaning in so that I might get a better view of the lines around her eyes.

"What am I supposed to be looking at?" I asked, leaning in.

I saw exactly what I was supposed to be looking at. Thin little stems, like baby's breath without the breath, branched out from the corners of her eyes, encroaching on her temples.

"I don't see anything," I said, and sat back.

You could argue that I was doing her a disservice by not saying anything. A response of "yes, I see of what you speak" might have made us both feel better as well as prevented her from inflicting this test on more of our friends. But she needed to vent. She insisted that her face was becoming a huge tell, that she didn't mind turning forty so much as she minded the assumptions other people made about her turning forty. They were starting to look at her like she should be married with kids and a house and matching towels. They made her feel like she should be running a company and wearing better shoes. Anything less inspired thinly veiled pity. Twenty-year-olds were starting to insist she exit elevators before them. Most horrifyingly, the adult she saw in the mirror when she emerged from the shower sometimes felt like a stranger.

I knew what she meant. And I empathized, for her fears were also my fears. But as much as I want to pause time for her, for me, for all of us, I know that's not possible. Chasing youth with our faces is a surefire way to never catch it. And if we set the surface of things aside—why would we want to? There is such strength and character and objective attractiveness written on my friend's face. You could say she looks young for her age because she does look young for her age, but mostly she looks more and more like her. She may not feel it every day, but she should at least feel it when we talk about it like this.

So I admitted that, actually, I could see the lines. She rolled her eyes, reveling in the confirmation. Then she casually floated the idea of needles. I told her what I would tell any woman as young as forty—if your face bothers you so much, invest some of that grown-up cash in better bathroom lighting. And maybe a couple of those masks that crack when you smile.

5

Why I Didn't Answer Your Email

KJ DELL'ANTONIA

I'm forty-seven years old.

Two days ago, when I was also forty-seven years old, you sent me an email, which I did not answer. I didn't answer it, in part, because I am forty-seven years old. My husband is forty-eight, and my children are fifteen, twelve, eleven, and eleven. They, too, did not answer your email, although I do not suppose that surprised you, as you didn't send them an email.

I appreciated your email. You are a person, who has written an email, and I am a person, who should reply to that email, one person to another. However, your email arrived on Wednesday afternoon, and just as I opened it, my almost-sixteen-year-old son came in. He wanted to describe to me an app he is in the process of developing. It was a gloriously detailed description, illustrated in fact, and I took it all in. I took him in, too, all almost-six-feet of him, all almost-driver of him, all almost-grown-up of him.

Then I settled in to really hash out the details, and examine the illustrations, because my almost-sixteen-year-old wanted my opinion, and then he wanted to tell me more, and then he showed me a funny article someone had sent him, and then I showed him a funny article someone had sent me, and then I explained that I had work to do, that I needed, in fact, to respond to your email, and also to write three thousand words in the next thirty-six hours. I've only written three hundred, I said.

Then you just have to do that again, he said, ten times.

This seemed to me very encouraging, and I said so, appreciatively, conveniently ignoring the fact that many of the words I had written were the wrong words, and in the wrong order, although I felt certain I had the right letters in there. I reapplied myself to my computer, where your email was open on the screen, and he left, and then he returned.

Actually, he said happily, you only have to do it again *nine* times.

I was so inspired by this that I abandoned your email, and all emails, and applied myself to my work. I would have replied to your email after a few hundred more words, I am certain, except that my eleven-year-old daughter came in, clutching some pieces of paper that I had earlier asked her to remove from the kitchen counter, because I had just accidently started to butter one of them. Oh, she said, that's okay. They're supposed to look old.

That explained the tea stains, and also the tea-stained kitchen sink. Now, the papers having dried, she proposed to read them to me. Dear Becky, she began, I take my pen in hand to tell you that I am well, but so afeared and worried, for we are going to the battle tomorrow.

She looked up. It's supposed to be a letter from Jeremiah, a soldier in in the Civil War, she explained, unnecessarily. Only a few hours earlier, I had typed Civil War letters for her brother, who is in the same class, and just a little before that, or maybe two years ago, I had listened to Civil War letters read by her older sister, and a little earlier still, just a few blinks of the eye, to historic missives drafted by the almost-sixteen-year-old who had just left the room. Those letters had had the exact same crumpled and match-burned edges and been stained with the exact same tea.

•   •   •

My eleven-year-old daughter read on, while I wondered where she found the matches. I am afraid the story of Jeremiah did not go well, and he ended his third letter, the one written after he was wounded in the stomach, by imploring Becky to hear his voice in the wind in the trees, reminding her to enjoy all the joys that life offered. Jeremiah's Civil War experience stood in stark contrast to that of Johnny, as penned by my youngest son. Johnny was a captain who had trained all his men perfectly and had plenty to eat and drink and was very excited about the battle, which he then enjoyed, thank you very much, dear Grandpa, with much love from Johnny.

Jeremiah's letters were very sad, and I said so. Was there, I inquired, perchance another letter, detailing Jeremiah's miraculous recovery?

No, my daughter said, gaily twirling around in her stocking feet on the wood floor. He got shot in the stomach, and that always kills you, because you can't remove a stomach.

I nodded. No, I agreed, you can't remove a stomach. Then she sat down next to me and put the poodle on her lap and started to discuss the parts of people that you could remove, even with a dull knife, a long time ago, back when people took the time to burn the edges of their letters before staining them with tea and dropping them in the nearest battlefield-adjacent mailbox. Fingers and toes, certainly; arms; even, a little surprisingly, legs. We spent some minutes discussing which of those things we would rather be without (toes, and maybe one leg or one hand but not both, because then how would you brush your hair, but maybe you could ride a bike if you had special handlebars). During this conversation, I did not answer your email.

I think that I would have answered your email if you had sent it earlier, by which I mean several years earlier, when these children were smaller and their conversation more repetitive. I would have been hidden in my office, a younger, more driven me, with the door closed and a big sign on it that said go away, instead of sitting as often I do now, in the middle of the house, an invitation to interruption. I would have put the contrast between Jeremiah and Johnny out of my mind and focused on the screen. Instead, after a lengthy discourse on dismembering delivered in the still-piping voice of my delicate fairy of a child, I found that I needed to go outside and look at the trees, not to listen for the voice of Jeremiah but because they were so compellingly green. I needed to walk aimlessly down the driveway, and then, filled with purpose, to the mailbox. There were no letters.

I also had to make dinner.

I almost answered your email later, after bedtime, which

is when I have often answered emails, yours and others. My laptop was conveniently, if precariously, perched on the stack of books on my bedside table. My husband was perched, less precariously, on his side of the bed, and he stretched out his legs and leaned back on his pillows and asked me if I'd given any thought to whether the chickens would need to be kept away from the apple trees after he sprayed them with something to keep the bugs away, from the trees, that is, not the chickens.

I had not, but what I was thinking about was the question the pediatrician had asked that morning, when I took my older daughter and my youngest son together for their annual checkup.

The question the pediatrician asked, very casually, was this: Have any family members died early from a cardiac event?

I thought about that, and asked, what's early?

Before fifty?

No, I said. Older, yes, but not before fifty. My husband's father died of a heart attack in his late sixties.

She nodded, as if that were perfectly acceptable. Not early, then. A cardiac event after fifty was punctual, perhaps, or even late, not a cause for alarm, not there, on her checklist. I wanted to ask her if early was inclusive of fifty—as in, is fifty itself early, or just fifty-one—but I refrained, and we moved on to screen time, water safety, and vaccinations, and then the appointment was over.

My husband and I moved on from talk of chickens and apple trees to the children's math grades, and the way they just take their socks off and leave them, inside out, no matter where they are. It was very convenient, how we were perched on the bed like that, and he was forty-eight, and still is, and I was forty-seven, and still am. I looked at the clock and saw that it was not as early as I thought, not for a lot of things, and so we turned off one light, but not both, and I did not answer your email.

Your email sat, I admit, among emails from bosses and editors and orthodontists, all through the next workday. My children were at school, and I had not yet managed to write three hundred words nine more times, or even six more times, although I was closing in on five. There were moments, certainly, when your email sang the siren song of procrastination, and I am sorry to tell you, but glad to say to myself, that I resisted.

I thought about answering your email in the afternoon, while my older daughter and I waited outside the school for her younger sister to finish a piano lesson. My daughter probably would not have minded. She is almost thirteen, and sometimes, when she sits in the house texting while I try to talk to her, I squirt her with the bottle I keep on the counter to spray the cats when they start scratching the back of the sofa. I could have answered your email then. I admit it. We could have sat there, in peaceful silence on the spring day, side by side on a bench, each staring at our phone. I had time to answer your email, and I did not.

Later, I needed to pick up a loaf of bread at a local restaurant, and while I was paying, someone called to place an order. The person who was taking my money was young, and alone, and she stopped with the register drawer out and my bills on the little shelf above the drawer, prior to making change. She leaned on her elbow on the counter, holding the phone with her shoulder, and very uncomfortably dealt with all that needed to be done for the invisible person contained within her ear instead of with me, the person who was standing directly in front of her. I think she would certainly have answered your email by now, whereas I have not. Instead, I took the bread and I went home and I made dinner, again, and then we all sat around the table and ate it.

I snuggled my youngest son at bedtime that night, because he asked, although I did not tell him a story, because it has been a while since he has asked for a story. I snuggled him even though your email was calling, and some part of me wanted to pull away from the tedium of bedtime and reply. Replying would have felt fresh and new, while bedtime felt old and stale, although it has grown far less demanding of late, with no more reading out loud and no more splashing baths, many of which I spent answering emails, which was fine, because there were so many bedtimes and so many baths, so very, very many of them, until suddenly there weren't, although there were still a lot of emails.

I would like to say I snuggled my son and did not give your email one single thought, but that would not be true, and it would also be rude, even though it is a state of mind to which many of us aspire. Instead, I hovered somewhere between mindful presence in the bedtime moment and awareness of your email and many others. I spend a lot of time in that gap, sometimes drafting mental responses to emails, which I am later surprised and dismayed to find I have not actually sent.

It is possible that I will answer your email later, in a few hours, or in a few years, when I am fifty-seven, and I will be so happy to have your email. We will trade words in our laptops and those words will again seem so real to me, a whole world in my laptop, where I live, sometimes, because there is so much that is seductive in there, where time moves fast and yet also never moves at all. I will take my laptop outside and

I will sit among the trees, listening for the voices of children who are no longer here, and I will answer your email.

It is also possible that I will not—that I, in fact, will never answer your email. If that is the case; if the people and the places and the things around me still press upon me with more urgency than your email and so many others, I hope that you will forgive me. I have already forgiven myself.

6

I Became an Actress at Thirty-Nine

JILL KARGMAN

I became an actress at thirty-nine. With stretch marks. With crow's-feet. With three pregnancies' worth of cellulite looking like Breakstone's cottage cheese on my thass, the heinous fusion of thigh plus ass. It was a dream come true—the acting, not the cellulite.

After always being in plays at college, it was a long-ass break till thirty-nine. Of course, as a college grad, I figured if I could press a button and pick a career, it would be onstage. But you can't just decide to be an actress and necessarily make it happen; in fact I remember saying to a friend, "I just want to act; I don't want to *be an actress*; I just want to act!" I truly felt like my motivations were never for fame and fortune but for the love of getting out there and playing characters. But you don't get to just go do it. Even the people you assume can, can't.

When I was a freshman, there was a senior who was the prettiest girl at Yale and I knew in my soul she was going to make it big. I was positive: she had it all—mesmerizing talent, the voice of an angel, legs for days. Two years later I ran into her, gorgeous as ever. Working at a restaurant in New York. *"Party of five? Right this way. . . ."* Holy shit: if she couldn't make it, I had zero chance.

While most performers are starry-eyed tits-on-stick in-génues with glossy head shots featuring their dewy, un-lined skin and perfect duck-lip pout, I figured with my un-Hollywood looks and penchant for workaholism, being a professional actress wasn't a red-carpeted path I should sashay down, since you can work your tail off auditioning and still never get roles. I figured I'd be waiting on people forever—waitressing tables and awaiting a call for that next self-taped reading. I didn't want to fuck fat casting directors, which is what I once thought was a ticket to stardom. I also knew that success in this world was not a meritocracy; there are Juilliard geniuses who languish and talent-free idiots who prevail. It wasn't fair! And that would drive me fucking crazy.

So I went to work as an assistant (read: Xerox whore) at *Interview* magazine and basically ate shit sandwiches for two years, doing the kind of cheese-danish-fetching clerical work I hear millennials feel above doing these days. It was so disheartening, because of course as you're running around in fifteen-degree weather to buy your boss cigarettes, you have no clue how this could possibly move your career forward. But the feces-panini years paid off. You don't realize it at the time, but one often learns by osmosis, and within a year and a half I was writing my own articles for *Interview* and other magazines. Work begets work, and as my twenties passed I found that I could juggle writing with raising my kids. I shat out three of them in four years, and I had what I call Placenta Brain, where I was so exhausted and hormonal, I would walk into a room and forget why I was going there. As a result, my ambition had this weird ebb and flow where I would have a burst of creativity and motivation, then I'd fall into an unproductive slump during the next pregnancy or recovery. I felt like I was knocked up for five years, basically. But as the babies turned into crawlers, then turned into zombie-walkers and finally, preschoolers, I figured I could work on my next book. I wound up writing a bunch during those chaotic years, and I could jam when I felt like it or be in mommy-mode when I didn't. And it was a balance that worked for me. For a while.

• • •

Fast forward: I'm thirty-five in the shower, gripped by a lingering ache: *Is this all there is?* Not regarding my acting fantasy per se, but just a general missing something. What exactly, I had no idea. I felt like a total asshole even thinking that because I knew I had a great life—hashtag blessed—and shouldn't feel like I needed any more than I already had. But I'd had a melanoma tumor the year before that left me with a foot-long scar on my thigh and an invisible one on my brain. I weirdly had a sudden and all-enveloping sense of urgency to sack up and do more. Try new things, act sillier, go nuts, feel free. I went skiing off a mountain with a parachute, for crying out loud. Jews don't do that shit! The adrenalized cheap thrills weren't enough, though—I realized I wanted to truly shift gears. But with three kids and responsibilities, it's hard to just shake the Etch A Sketch of life and have a clean slate.

I remember around that time a bunch of moms were hanging out after a pal's birthday lunch. Someone said, "The freaky thing about getting older is that the funnel is closing." I asked WTF that meant, and she explained that when you're young you can decide to do anything and options are *wiiiide*-open, and as we age, our lives are poured down a funnel and options narrow. *Por ejemplo*, with all the interminable years of medical school, hospital residencies, specialty boards, etc., it's pretty unlikely someone pushing forty could decide to be a doctor.

In a sudden whirl of claustrophobia, I started hyperventilating. *Was she right?* Okay . . . maybe being a doctor . . . but what about . . . acting? It was not even a fully formed "dream" of mine, because I never would've had the balls to dream it. It's not like I had to learn how to hold a scalpel 'n' shit. Art (or quirky TV) isn't saving lives, right? In a weird way, though, it did save mine.

At thirty-seven I was a copywriter at Ogilvy for the production company Piro (Tim *Pi*per and Daniel *Ro*senberg's company, hence the name) literally doing maxi pad and adult diaper commercials. One tagline I pitched: *"With Poise®, Urine the clear!"* Daniel and Tim were so amazing and hilarious to work with, and I felt understood. Plus the collaborative aspect of working in an office versus at home with my Karglings for eleven years banging out novels on my tragic CB2 TV-dinner table in the corner of my bedroom felt invigorating.

After one particularly hysterical goofball brainstorm session that left us all in stitches, Daniel asked if I'd ever want to do television. I mean, of course I would, but one doesn't just snap her soy-sauce-bloated fingers and make that happen.

But they had ideas. And more importantly, they had faith in me. One thing led to another and we wound up making a guerilla sizzle reel for an R-rated talk show, kind of like a late-night program, but in the morning. It was called *Wake the Fuck Up!* No saccharine smiles and coffee mug bullshit. I'd drink from a straw an entire pot of coffee, sitting in my pajamas with hair like a rat's nest. I'd get ready while on camera. I'd do the weather report by opening my window: IT'S FUCKING FREEZING!

Piro sent it to networks, and Andy Cohen wanted to meet. In the room at 30 Rock that day was Lara Spotts, who would become my writing partner, showrunner, and all-around goddess. Together, we developed what became *Odd Mom Out*, a scripted comedy about trying to fit in on New York's Upper East Side. Now, say what you will about Bravo and their slate of mostly reality shows that often include catfights and people with implants weeping, but NO other channel on your dial would ever pluck someone pushing forty from obscurity? from regular life? and have them star in a TV show. The cool thing is that Bravo always does that. A word was even coined for the phenomenon: *Bravolebrity!*

Suddenly, while many women around the age of forty were freaking that the best was behind them, I was proof that is not the case. I was proof that it's never too late to switch shit up, and the key is having just a couple of people who believe you can. But even more importantly, *you* need to believe it. True, without Daniel and Tim pushing me along, I probably never would have had the balls. But why not? Because women tend to think in terms of that ever-tightening funnel. Our boobs drop and our asses widen and the world tells us we've peaked. But here's the special secret: we're more productive and better than ever because by forty, we know who we are.

I have no doubt that I would have been a failure as a performer at twenty-two. Maybe I had higher tits and no cellulite, but honestly, who the fuck cares. When we are young, we are diluted versions of ourselves. We become balsamic reductions as we age—our very best parts distilled and clarified. Which is why they make needlepoint pillows that say aging is great like wine or cheese—and not like bananas, but that's besides the point. The key is that now I am a fully formed person! Mistakes have been made, relationships terminated, and the cocoon surrounding my forty-plus-year-old self feels like trusty battle-worn armor for my soul. Time gives you that. Things don't bother me as much as they used to. When I was a new mom who didn't breastfeed, I literally had a nursing nazi say "SHAME ON YOU!" and I walked around the corner and burst into tears. Years later when I had my third and some asshole started pontificating that if I don't nurse, my son wouldn't be as smart, I replied with a smile, "Oh, I was bottle-fed and IQs don't come higher than mine!" and walked off. Little did I know, honing my ability to not give a shit was a tool that would come in handy in my new career.

When *Odd Mom Out* premiered, I was beaming with pride and flattered by the critical praise. But there were also ego-balloon needle pricks by Twitter trolls who said that I was too wrinkly to be on television. That I had snaggleteeth. That my hair was too thin. That I looked like Marilyn Manson's daughter. Of course some stung for a split second, but then I honestly did not care at all. Because I'm old enough to embrace the look I have (though I did get some help in the chopper department with Invisalign!) and not give a shit about superficial comments. But in my twenties? Oh, I'd have casually walked to my roof and swan-dove off, Louganis-style. I would just not have been able to deal with those comments without the lovely shield of crocodile-thick skin that I developed over time. In fact, I truly don't know how all these young actresses do it. They strike me as so brave. Perhaps their generation knows that with the internet comes the basement-dwelling assholes, and dismisses them casually as part of the game.

Now, at forty-three, I can honestly say I feel like I'm in the best part of my life—my kids are not laying cable in their Huggies and they've become my favorite people in the world. They go to sleepaway camp, which is like a defibrillator on my sixteen-year marriage, giving it a welcome electric jolt. This summer my awesome husband and I got to pole-vault back in time over our thirties to what it was like dating in our twenties, when we were boyfriend and girlfriend and there were no kids barging in and ruining sex with their boner-wilting shrieks. I now have only my sister-level friends around me, no toxic holdovers kept around because of inertia. Your forties afford you the opportunity to cull your circle. As they say aboard the *World War Z* Atlantic ship fleet, all nonessential people must go.

And the acting? Well, here's a funny twist.

After my third season of *Odd Mom Out* wrapped, my agent sent me to a round-robin of casting directors in Los Angeles. Remember my nightmare of obese, rapey, cigar-smoking men with casting couches? Well, all eight meetings were with women. Cool, badass, amazing women. In their fifties. When I said I probably was not the typical new face sent in to meet with them—the Crypt Keeper compared to the parade of Barbies teetering in—I was told that actually many of the women in their forties in the business had been around for so long, while I, coming out of fucking nowhere, was "fresh." Not a description you hear very often in your mid-forties. Turns out there was a benefit to not acting out of college. And for me, personally, I don't think I could have brought much to roles then because I hadn't lived anyway. The tunnel of vision at that age, the ambition to succeed, is so narrow. And then it opens. You know who you wind up with, you know who you are, you know where you're going. So maybe the funnel *does* tighten, but all you have to do is turn it upside down: it's all how you frame it. And if you have one artistic bone in your body, I say pull it like a wishbone and go for it—there's so much more of you to pump into your work now. There are more laughs to draw from, more manic sobfests you've endured. The colors are brighter because you appreciate those ROYGBIVs more after the emotional storm clouds and the hurricanes of turmoil. There is more rage to channel from the injustices of the world that youth often tunes out. There's more joy to embrace from what we now know is the fleeting cackle of a sugar-cracked toddler or a baby's cuddle.

I've always thought art should be what is clawing its way out of you, scratching for that canvas or computer or camera. For me, holding up a fun-house mirror to the world with writing is what makes me not fear aging. No one watches my show because they think I'm pretty; they watch 'cause it makes them laugh. And you're supposed to look silly in a fun-house mirror! A regular one is boring. Leave those to the seflie-snapping youngsters.

The single most important lesson I've learned in my life so far is . . .

"To be quiet."

—*Jessica Lahey*

"My life isn't a dress rehearsal; you have got to do what you want; make the changes you want now while you can."

—*Julie Klam*

"Put your phone down and kiss your partner good-bye; greet your kids at the door; listen to your friends; and stroke your grunting, purring animals with your full attention. Life is only the collection of moments that make it up. You really don't want to miss them because you're waiting for some bigger or better or less annoying thing to happen. As I used to say when my babies were babies: There is no after putting on the snowsuit. There is only putting on the snowsuit."

—*Catherine Newman*

"Everything looks better, feels better, and is *way* more manageable in the morning."

—*Lee Woodruff*

"The single most important lesson I've learned at this point in my life is that happiness is an inside job and an every day job. I think about how can I be happy every. single. day. If I do one good, kind thing for myself each day then I'm more content and more equipped to spread joy to the people I love."

—*Veronica Chambers*

7

Inheritance
and
Tip of My Tongue

JENA SCHWARTZ

Inheritance

Somewhere, a daughter mourns her father
and a mother digs in the dirt where
her daughter played long ago. Somewhere
a father looks at his hands and remembers
the man he was when his daughter was young.
A daughter reaches for words from air
and a mother touches the paintings

her daughter made all those years ago
before she died. Somewhere a father
is reading a book and a daughter is writing
a poem and a mother is sitting on her deck
where the flowering trees have sprung
blossoms overnight and will fall as quickly.
Somewhere, somehow, fathers and daughters
and daughters and mothers hold fast
to each other's likenesses, until who came
before and who left first becomes a blur
of spring color, a riot of grief and blessing
and everything else that will have to wait.
Call me from the afterlife, I want to call out
before she hangs up, my daughter calling
from the canyon's edge where she dangled
her feet, where she overheated, where
she glimpsed, for the first time, how vast
her inheritance.

Tip of My Tongue

I woke with a poem
on the tip of my tongue.
But first—a kitchen, a teenager,
head heavy against forearms
on the table, an offering as I toasted
her bagel and gave her neck
a gentle squeeze as if to say, *I get it.*
First, a fifth-grader who last night slid
soap bubbles onto the tip of his tongue,
trying to catch the ineffable
between dinner and dishes,
the drive to the bus, a shared moment
over an Instagram video
of a toddler mimicking her mama
and making me remember
how she came out singing
in ways I never could have taught her.

The poem would wait until later—
there was a household to tend to,
calls to make and bills to pay,

a path in the woods whispering my name,
my own parents' house a mile away standing
between me and my old, young self
who didn't have wrinkles or flab
or the wisdom to know that she didn't know,
who was porcelain sure she knew who she was
but buried grenades in her belly
and the black sky of a new moon
in her crescent-shaped eyes.

That morning, I pulled into my own driveway
and noticed my car wasn't there.
Oh, I'm not home, I thought,
as if this was the most normal realization.
Where was I, then? That was the question
I had spent all those years walking over,
a land mine covered with wildflowers.
From the bedroom window where I sat
alone after the business of the morning,
the busy morning settling around me,
the nascent leaves outside growing
toward the full expression of another summer,
two mourning doves walked the seam
of the neighbor's shed

and I watched from the windows
as they bickered and preened,
a morning ritual for the ones
who mate for life
before flying off in different directions
for the day.

I turned to look over my left shoulder,
at my wife whose body wrapped around mine
was the answer to a question
I didn't even know I was asking.
And finally there came this space,
this stillness, breath like a coordinate—
You are here.
Roll the poem over your tongue now,
and take the bittersweet of it like a garnet
disguised as gravel on the path
of your becoming.
It's all yours.

8

Adaptation of Life

KATE BOLICK

All of us tell stories about our pasts. No other material seems so wholly at our command. But when the telling reaches a certain size, the scales tilt, and the story takes over. Recently I learned this firsthand, by publishing an entire book about my past. Now, when I turn to look back at forty, the blur of selling, then writing, then promoting that book nearly blots out the rest of my now half-over decade.

That it was my first book may have something to do with its outsize impact on my forties, but who knows. I've always written, first in the usual child way, then as a college poet, and after that, as a freelance writer and full-time editor at various magazines and newspapers. In adulthood, I longed to know again the kinetic sensation I'd once felt composing poems: the tight, bright flare of an image materializing as a fully formed phrase; the tumble of rhythmic progression that followed; the frisson of analyzing whatever it was my subconscious was trying to say. I'd never minded that my poems made little sense to other people. I believed in the idea of apprenticeship and trusted that someday I'd reach the elusive next level where what I wrote communicated meaning to others. This achievement would be my success and arrival.

I never did get there. In May 1996, the year after I finished college, my mother died unexpectedly of breast cancer, at fifty-two. I was consumed with grief, and for the first time, I couldn't find the words to express what I felt. My wordlessness was unbearable, as if I'd been locked inside a metal box, left to look at my life transpiring through a narrow slit at the top. How would I get out, talk again to other people, continue to find my way as an adult? Suddenly poetry seemed like the most preposterous thing I'd ever heard of, effete and inadequate, a trail of dissolving vapors when what I needed was a firm, sturdy ladder. In high school I'd had a job making fried dough at an amusement park, and one night my coworker actually announced, "I quit," untied his apron, leaped over the counter, and jogged away into the night. And so just like that, I quit poetry. To climb out of this box and communicate with other people, I would learn how to write sentences, and paragraphs. Ladder rungs.

It was all very dramatic, in the way of an early twenty-something, and yet enduringly real. I still don't know: Was my total renunciation of poetry fallout from my bereavement, or my knowing, deep down, that at the end of the day it was something I loved but wasn't very good at, and I needed to get on with other things in order to become a self-supporting adult?

Vapors or ladder rungs. Whatever I chose to muck around with in my private hours, I definitely needed to get a job. That June, I applied for and received an assistant position at the *Atlantic* magazine, in Boston. Eventually I became a literary editor on the magazine's website. Learning how to edit was deeply engaging, and it consoled me to be acquiring a concrete skill, like cutting hair or tending bar, that I could carry forward and always use to find employment.

In the spring of 2000, when I twenty-seven, I felt ready to try writing prose myself. I decided to write a short, lyrical homage to Filene's Basement (an historic department store I loved that's since gone out of business). To my great surprise, while writing it, something like poetry happened—the homage morphed into a personal essay about shopping at the

Basement with my mother, and her death, which appears as abruptly to the reader as it had to me four years prior.

Once finished, I worried that the mashup of central concerns—clothes shopping, mothers and daughters, breast cancer—was a treacly combination of fluff and sentiment. I submitted it to the magazine anyhow and was thunderstruck when they accepted it. When it came out, in the January 2001 issue, I received emails from readers saying they'd been moved. I was astonished. Finally, I'd done it: I'd communicated what I'd felt in a way that could be understood by another person.

It was an extraordinary sensation, this rush of intimate connection once removed. I wanted to experience it again, but I couldn't think of anything else worth writing about.

Instead of writing more personal essays, I studied them. It intrigued me to unravel the ways in which people choose to talk about their pasts, assuming various postures and tones, seemingly divulging every last juicy detail to the reader, or showing only part of the story. For a while I had a column for the *Boston Globe*, reviewing memoirs.

Life clipped along, vivid and ordinary. I moved to New York, got a master's degree in cultural criticism, applied for jobs, worked in offices, fell in and out of love, made new friends, lost others, moved apartments. Along the way, I published several more short, personal essays, and felt closer to that longed-for poetry-like sensation my first essay had produced. But the impulse to write such pieces was intermittent, which was frustrating but ultimately fine. Once again, I believed in the idea of apprenticeship, and trusted someday I'd find a subject worth sinking into, that would be meaningful to me and also to others, though this time around I'd be writing nonfiction, not poems. If sentences and paragraphs were ladder rungs, then journalism—researching, reporting, interviewing—would provide the vertical rails.

The vexing thing about a self-declared apprenticeship is that you never know when it will end, or what form its ending will take. Sometimes I was desperately impatient, watching my peers vault into leagues of accomplishment I might never know, and I worried often that like my mother, I would die unexpectedly, whether of breast cancer or something else, before I could accomplish anything at all. This tension between my constant pushing-forward and fear-of-death gave my thirties an uncanny intensity; with each passing day, I was a step closer to one fate or the other, and which would it be? My mother had found that first lump in her breast when she was thirty-seven, finally received a correct diagnosis at thirty-nine, and undergone her first mastectomy at forty.

And then it was me who was thirty-nine, and as if out

of nowhere, my apprenticeship ended. It was the summer of 2011, and I was living half the time in Los Angeles, the rest in Brooklyn, working as culture editor of a home-decor magazine, and writing freelance on the side. The *Atlantic* asked me to report and write a cover story about changing marriage trends, in the first person, drawing on my own experiences and observations as a woman who'd never been married. It was the biggest assignment I'd ever been given. I said yes immediately, elated and terrified. Did I have the chops to pull it off? How would I even begin? I emailed a close friend, a journalist who'd written quite a few cover stories, asking her advice, and she responded saying she was too busy to help and too jealous anyhow, that she'd "kill to have an *Atlantic* cover story." My first glimpse of the sordid underbelly of "success": the jealousy of others.

For eight weeks I reported and researched in my off hours, taking five different plane trips, conducting interviews with economists, psychiatrists, sociologists, and historians, as well as single women and single mothers of various ages, trying to understand why Americans were marrying less and later than ever before. Quickly the piece turned into an exploration of the growing singles demographic. It wasn't a personal essay by a long shot. Though I was, as instructed, drawing on my own experiences and observations, I wasn't "telling my story" so much as employing the narrative "I" as a device to hook and then guide the reader through a mountain of complicated material. The final result was more than double the length I'd been assigned. I called it "All the Single Ladies."

After I filed the story, my editor called to say they wanted to feature my face on the magazine's cover. I said sure, but I felt dread. Magazine covers are the province of famous models and actors and politicians; one benefit of being a writer is remaining unseen. I have never liked being looked at. More unsettling, I knew that pairing my face with my words would influence readers' reactions in ways I couldn't predict. And yet, as a magazine editor myself, I understood the reasoning behind the decision: I wasn't merely reporting on this demographic shift, I also embodied it. Because of the stigma against single women, who historically have been told something is "wrong" with them, most readers would immediately conduct a Google search to see what I look like, and draw their own conclusions. A photograph of a real-life single woman who appears perfectly content with her lot would be arresting and sell more magazines. It was cynical, but not untrue.

In early September I drove to a studio in Los Angeles for the photo shoot. A stylist zipped me into a navy lace dress, a makeup artist darkened my eyes with heavy black liner, and a photographer instructed me to fold my arms into an

I-couldn't-care-less pose, then told me exactly which part of my lip to curl, and how. Everybody was nice, but I felt extraordinarily uncomfortable being at the center of such an elaborate production, and even more so when I learned that the real model, a gorgeous young woman who'd been hired for the secondary shots—a stiletto through a wedding cake, something like that—was in fact out of sorts, that I hadn't been imagining things. She'd been told she would be on a magazine cover. It was hard to resist the temptation to apologize and explain I knew she was the cover-worthy one around here, not me.

Later that week, my editor emailed me a PDF of the photograph. I nearly threw up. What was this baggy-eyed, sunspotted, acne-scarred, mole-ridden, slightly asymmetrical regular-person face doing where a model's should be? My editor said I'd feel better once the image was retouched. He was right: I'd never looked so good, or less like myself. When I showed it to my journalist friend on my iPhone, she blanched and said, "So, now you're going to have your single girl moment."

The article appeared in the November 2011 issue and immediately went viral, a phenomenon I'd never thought twice about, so wasn't prepared for. The circus of scrutiny was totally disorienting. I'd been working in journalism for fifteen years, all that time anonymous, and now readers were emailing me death threats, as if I'd invented the idea of not getting married and was recruiting helpless rubes to join my cult. Hot takes mushroomed across the internet. Trolls took to Twitter, citing my "hairy hamster arms" (among other physical flaws) for why I wasn't married. As a reporter, I was contractually bound to appear on television and radio programs to discuss the story I'd written, but more than a few interviewers behaved as if I were a spokesperson representing a movement and the article was my manifesto. It was absurd. Fundamental to my understanding of being single and being married is that both states are fungible. A wife can wake up married one morning and by lunch learn her husband wants a divorce. A confirmed bachelorette can walk around the corner and meet the love of her life, or just change her mind and decide to download a dating app after all.

But good things happened, too. I received scores of emails from single women thanking me for making them feel less invisible. Oprah almost had me on as a guest. Sony optioned the TV rights. Six months later I'd walk into an office in Hollywood and watch a three-minute "zinger reel" of highlights from my every talk show appearance, which was used to introduce the pitch meetings for a sitcom about a single woman named Kate Bobek. (CBS commissioned a pilot but didn't make the show.) My face appeared on several more covers, here and abroad, for stories about my story.

Out of nowhere, I was a "success"!

But was I, really? Of course I'd dreamed of success, but I'd never envisioned anything like this. I'd hoped to eventually find my way as a writer, and if I was lucky, write books. Instead, I was temporarily internet-famous as the spokeswoman for a nonexistent movement based on a mistaken identity. We hear about impostor syndrome, and how women feel it more often than men, but this was different. This was the sensation of living out somebody else's fantasy. I wasn't being lauded for what I'd written—I was a reality star, a circus freak, a spectacle. Even after the moment had passed, and I was living a more private life again, the din of those several months continued to ring in my ears for at least as many years.

Before you think of me as someone who's protesting too much, or a writer asking for sympathy in response to attention willingly sought, I should be clear that I was doing two things. I was being naive about the costs of my increased visibility, even as I was savvy enough to know that this exposure was also my chance to get a book deal. If you're me, the realization that you can be both naive and savvy at once is something you might only figure out after spending half a decade untangling the consequences.

This morning I clicked back through my Google calendar to 2011 to double-check the series of events that came next, and my heart began to race—with fear, but of what? Everything is in the past. And yet it all feels blindingly contemporaneous, as if this day, right now, isn't in fact bounded by morning and night but encompasses every moment of the last six years, as if there's no such thing as a past. As if everything between 2011 and today is an ever-presence.

Possibly this sense of ever-presence is because my past six years actually have contained an uncommon amount of activity, and I'm only now slowing down. But then I think of friends my age, and wonder if this is also just the feeling of being in one's forties. No matter the circumstance—wealthy, broke, married, single—it seems everyone is exhausted, distracted, scrambling. All through childhood and adolescence and young adulthood we were moving forward, toward the future, trying to be what we wanted to become. And then, at some undetermined point, we crashed into the understanding that the future is here, right now, whether or not it's the one we hoped for. We each made a series of decisions, and here is the result.

When I mused about this to a friend who's about to turn fifty, she mentioned a study that shows forty-five/forty-six tends to be the nadir of women's self-reported happiness scores. It's the multiple-whammy of maximum workload, child rearing, home building, and parents aging. "One is IN HARNESS pretty much constantly in one's forties," she wrote me in an email. "It's just task after task after task. I am hoping that my fifties will include a tiny bit more romping in the grass and voyaging abroad!"

At the same time, none of us have ever been so powerful, or as interesting. C, my best friend from high school, who'd basically never taken a day off work, stepped down from her executive position at a global retail company and spent a year traveling the world. M reinvented herself as a feast maker, and then again as a multimedia producer. R, who's always loved horses, answered a want ad and now works part-time at a stable when she's not teaching children with special needs and making her own art. Others are full professors at world-class universities, experts in their fields.

I suppose there are people out there who feel they've "arrived," or that they have this phase of life all figured out, but I've never met them. Or maybe I met one or two along the way, and they were insufferable or merely boring. Everyone I know my age feels some variation of flummoxed by the growing realization that we are no longer truly young, and never will be again, which is in turn paradoxically counterbalanced by relief over not having to be young anymore. It's sort of like with acne: when you're a teenager, all the grown-ups promise your skin will get better, but in truth it never really goes away and becomes what the dermatologist calls "adult acne." Other mistruths include that you'll get more confident and stop caring what other people think. As far as I can tell, these glories are reserved for menopause and rock stars. Until then, you're sunk. That is, if I'm any indication. The older and more so-called accomplished I get, the less sure of anything I am.

For good or for ill, while facing down this slowly dawning vista of self-doubt, I began to write my first book. It went like this: In November 2011, I wrote a book proposal. The book would be something of a precursor to the *Atlantic* cover story—my years as a straight, white, unmarried adult woman here in this new millennium—but intimate, though not a straight-up "confessional" memoir, rather, a calibrated hybrid of memoir, biography, history, and cultural criticism. Central to my coming-of-age as an adult had been the stories I'd told myself about other women, which I'd pieced together by reading the stories they'd told about themselves in novels, poems, essays, letters, and diaries, as well as the stories others told about them in biographies, autobiographies, and scholarly texts. I would tell *that* story: the story of my single life shaped by the stories of single lives that came before me.

In January 2012, my agent sent the proposal out to publishers. At the end of that month, I signed a book deal. That same evening, I went on a second date with S, a man I'd recently met over social media. At the time, his most salient feature—to me—was his relative youth: almost thirty-two to my pushing forty. I liked him instantly, but I fully expected our age difference to become an obstacle soon enough and figured we'd jump off that bridge when we came to it.

In the months that followed, I embarked on writing a book about my years as a single woman while also starting a new relationship that soon snowballed into something serious and called into question my supposed singleness. Meanwhile, because I was drawing on my own life, which naturally included my teens, twenties, and thirties, I spent an inordinate amount of time reflecting at length on my past, a highly unpleasant exercise that had the doubly adverse effect of making the past seem eerily present. For the two years it took to write the book, I felt an often dizzying and sometimes nauseating attitude toward myself and my own history. It's bad enough to go through your own mistakes at the time— but to relive them? Tedium at best.

At last, the manuscript was nearly finished. By then, the fall of 2014, S and I were still dating. I couldn't decide: Should I mention in the book this man I'd been seeing for two years now, and risk giving the narrative what seemed perilously close to the traditional "happy ending" I was trying to subvert, even though for all I knew we'd break up before the book came out? I decided it was best to be transparent, and that I would mention him. After some deliberation, I called the book *Spinster: Making a Life of One's Own*.

Next, in an odd twist of déjà vu, my publisher announced their decision to photograph me for the book's cover. This time I said no. I had many reasons. For one, though a photo of an average-looking middle-aged non-actress/model wouldn't contribute to our contemporary plague of unattainable beauty standards, I was still in my fertile years, if at the tail end of them, and I didn't like the idea of capitalizing on my relative youth in order to make a sale. Moreover, I wasn't sure I could bear that kind of public scrutiny again. I pictured diet books emblazoned with beaming women triumphantly holding measuring tapes to show how much weight they'd lost. Wouldn't putting me on the cover convey the same sort of message, as if I were holding up myself as an example to be emulated, rather than exploring a topic through the lens of my personal experience? Finally, I worried that if I were on the cover of my book, nobody would take it, or me, seriously. I would no longer be a writer, but a commodity, a persona.

My publisher insisted. The only way they could sell a

book called *Spinster* was if the author was shown on the cover owning the word. I relented. What followed—the marketing and promotion—was stranger still.

There I was, on an actual book cover, my forty-two-year-old self posed demurely on a marigold velvet settee, wearing a tight-fitting turquoise neoprene dress and black suede heels the stylist had brought to the shoot, hair cascading past my shoulders in a glorious tumble of Photoshopped shine, looking to all the world as if I'm besotted with a cup of tea, as if indeed I want to *marry* that cup of tea.

There I was, in real life, still forty-two, then forty-three, then forty-four, trotting about promoting and defending a book about the consequences of prior decades as though it represented everything true and current, leaving me rhetorically caught between the very recent past that I had narrated, and the present, which with each passing day made my prior selves seem ever more distant. Meanwhile, I was also learning what it means not just to wait to have children, but to authoritatively and conscientiously blow through my last remaining years of fertility, while also talking about these highly personal matters in an authoritative manner on NPR.

(Also, I got breast cancer, but that's a whole other story. I'm fine now.)

And yet, that book has brought me into contact with

readers and other writers all over the world, drawing me into discussions and experiences that make my life feel bigger than I ever thought it could be, and more purposeful. I'm working on another book. I'm asked to write essays like this one.

I suspect that the terror of self-exposure is never going to vanish entirely for me, however. I'm like a stand-up comic with stage fright—I understand the world best when I'm writing about it in the first person, but I can't bear the vulnerability that comes with publication. Even writing this essay, which reads as so orderly and matter-of-fact, was a many-weeks-long psychological ordeal. It sickened me to meet the blank page only to discover that the pleasures of my forties—the richest, most wholly realized period of my life so far—had been eclipsed by professional anxieties I had no desire to revisit. Tough luck; my brain refused to focus on anything else.

And yet, though I've never found writing to be therapeutic, already, typing these final words, I feel lighter than I have for quite a while.

I could laugh. I've often heard it said that one should write what feels most difficult, and now that I have, I see I absolutely needed to recount my trial-by-fire initiation into the full-time writing life in order to take full possession of where I've landed. If I hadn't, I might not have recognized what may be among the great gifts of the forties: at long last having the maturity, and the ability, to see the ways in which our previous and current selves collide with and inform each other, even talk to each other. I still want, very much, to communicate meaning to other people. But I see now that what I'm doing here, in these pages, is equally as valuable.

9

There's a Metaphor Here

ALLISON WINN SCOTCH

My husband and I had planned to celebrate our thir-teenth anniversary in Mexico with our children and closest friends. Instead, he drove me to physical therapy due to a devastating injury from two weeks prior that meant I couldn't walk and I couldn't drive. There's a metaphor there, to be sure. But we'll get to that later.

I heard my bone crack before I felt it. At least, that's how I remember it. Crack first. Pain next. Probably, if I were think-ing clearly or if my memory were able to rewind in slow mo-tion like you can do on a DVR, the two—crack, pain—would fold on top of each other so that they were indistinguishable, braided together as one. But in my mind, it was *crack*, then agony.

When the doctors explained that I'd sheared off three-quarters of an inch of my *tibial plateau* (this is the bone that connects your shin to your knee and, I learned, one of the most important bones in the body for load bearing), I thought, *Oh yes, that's what that sound was. The sound of bone splitting into a million pieces.* But in the moment, it never occurred to me that my body was so fragile, so easily shattered. After all, I was a mother. The last time I'd taken a sick day was five years earlier when the flu slayed me in my tracks. Though I was forty-one, I was in arguably the best shape of my life. In my twenties, fitness had been about a number on a scale, a size on the back of a pant label. In my thirties, it had been about bouncing back from my pregnancies. In my forties, I was in shape for me and had a newfound sense of ownership of my body. I was running five or so miles a few times a week; I was toying with the notion of a lifelong aspiration of entering a marathon; I was (I felt like I was) invincible.

I'd grown up skiing but it hadn't been a love affair. Rather, it had been something that my parents enjoyed, and my older brother was zealous about, so I was stuffed into down overalls and bulky sweaters, offered hand warmers and itchy hats, and later, thanks to cool '90s technology, heated boots (which only worked part of the time). Throughout middle school and high school, I grudgingly took the ski bus up to the mountain each weekend. The bus rides were more thrilling for me than the slopes—flirting with boys, drinking Jolt Cola, and listening to boom boxes blasting with music we thought made us look more sophisticated. Eventually, I suppose out of habit, I became an excellent skier despite my aversion to the cold and to throwing myself down a mountain at top speeds with the wind chapping my cheeks and lips.

In adulthood, with no mandated weekend ski buses and few required family trips, I retired my Volkls, content to say, "I used to be a skier, but no longer." Then I met my husband, Adam, who grew up in New Hampshire and loved skiing as intensely as I loved sitting in the condo. For the first eight years of our marriage, I begged off ski trips and sent him off with his brother or friends without me. He always invited me—would have preferred me to come actually. It would have been something we shared, something we did as a unit, but I was happy staying warm and dry; I was happy without bruised shins from ill-fitting ski boots, without bracing myself against a frigid wind on a wobbly ski lift.

After we had children, he still asked me to join him, but by then, my pettier complaints about skiing had given way to graver concerns: *What if I get hurt?* My father was a neurosurgeon, and I grew up listening to catastrophic tales of woe, avalanches, broken necks, head-on collisions with trees. In high school, a boy a year ahead of me was paralyzed in a ski jump gone apocalyptically wrong. Once I became a parent, my concern over injury (or worse), both skiing related and otherwise, magnified: I got anxious on flights without my family, I fretted that lumps and bumps would prove cancerous. It wasn't that I was personally worried about death or a decimating injury exactly; it was that I worried about leaving my children behind, leaving my family unable to cope without me.

And thus each time Adam would set off on a ski trip and invite me along or ask if we could plan one for our family, and I'd cock my head and say, either to myself or aloud (usually both): *What if I'm in a terrible accident? Then what? Who will run our house? Who will take care of everything? How on earth will you carry on?* He'd look at me and laugh and say: "You won't get hurt. That's crazy. Come on, it will be fun."

Eventually, around when my children were seven and five, and because I didn't want my kids to be the type of kids who didn't know how to ski or grow up fearing adventure, I acquiesced. Maybe I'd been wrong. Maybe this actually *would be* fun. Maybe it wasn't all that dangerous. Besides, mothers took one for the team all the time; that was practically the subtitle of motherhood. I'd done plenty of other things that I didn't want to or didn't enjoy simply for the benefit of my children and my family. What was one more to add to my list?

It was the very first run of our long weekend in Colorado. We'd been skiing together as a family for three years now, and Adam had been right. It *was* fun! Maybe I *wouldn't* get hurt!

It was a perfect spring morning, and the skies were cloudless and blue, the temperatures warm. I'd been tired that morning, sluggish from staying up with the kids who wanted to watch late-night movies with their cousins whom they hadn't seen in months. Or maybe I was getting sick. I couldn't differentiate anymore between fatigue and illness. I considered opting out of the morning, sitting in the condo *by myself* and just . . . doing nothing. But the kids were whining about attending ski school, and I figured I should (and could) push through—that if I skipped out, then they'd think that they could, too.

We dropped the kids at ski school, and my brother and Adam charted our course on the mountain map. A little traverse to a bunny hill to a lift that would take us to the good stuff: the black diamonds. I dropped my skis on the packed snow and stepped into them so I could push off and chase my brother, his wife, and Adam, who were already off and figuratively running. My binding wasn't sticking. I slapped snow off my heel with my pole and tried again. I popped my boot in and out a few times until I figured that it was in there well enough. I'd learned to deal with little shortcuts like this, those *well enough* moments because most of my life was juggling being adequate at everything so that no one felt slighted.

Benign neglect.

My kids were thriving under that philosophy; surely, my binding could, too.

I pushed off onto the traverse and caught up with my sister-in-law. My legs felt too heavy; I debated, again, calling it a day. Then, three minutes into the run, just as we started down the crest of a small slope to the lift, my left ski came off, then my right ski inverted and took my leg with it, twisting it like a Raggedy Ann doll. I remember seeing my ski careening toward me at an obscene angle, and then I heard the *crack*.

I lay splattered on the snow screaming, my leg distorted at a right angle to my body, consumed by a level of pain I'd never experienced. Though because I am a mother who never allows herself a sick day, another voice inside of me was saying: "Calm down, calm down! Don't embarrass yourself, what if this is nothing?" Adam had skied ahead with my brother, but my sister-in-law heard my shrieks and doubled back. A kind volunteer EMT stopped and phoned ski patrol, and my sister-in-law called Adam and my brother, who hiked up the mountain to find me. By then, I was strapped on a toboggan, and was soon taken down the mountain and placed in an ambulance.

They couldn't give me pain meds until they took my X-ray. The pain was so severe that I was shaking on the X-ray table, unable to control my limbs as shock set in and took with it my muscle control. I kept apologizing to the technician. *"I'm sorry, I'm sorry, I'm sorry. I'm trying to hold still. I know I'm making your job harder."* I lay there and again wondered if I weren't being overdramatic, if I weren't going to be terribly embarrassed by all of this in about an hour when they gave me an Aleve and said: *Well, sweetie, you sprained it, just elevate it and give it some ice.*

I knew I wasn't prone to hysterics. There were those concerns about plane crashes, true, but I'd been so well-conditioned to ignore my own needs for someone else's that I truly couldn't decipher what was real pain and what wasn't, what was seemingly hysterical and what was justified.

A nurse arrived shortly after my X-ray and hooked some tubes into my nostrils for oxygen and finally brought me some blessed pills and also an IV drip to alleviate my agony with its very own button that I could push at my leisure when I felt like I was going to die. I apologized (again) to her: *"I'm so sorry, I couldn't keep still for the technician. I'm so sorry for needing these pills."*

I was. I was genuinely embarrassed for needing the help, for inconveniencing these people whose job it was to heal me. The nurse smiled kindly and said, "Oh, sweetie, once you see your X-ray, you'll understand."

Here's how things worked in my household: I did most of the shit. Ineloquently phrased, yes, but true all the same. I love my husband. We are happy and we are stable and we are partners. And I don't want this to go sideways and have anyone misconstrue that. But when it comes down to the nitty-gritty—the scheduling, the school forms, the home-work packets, the sports car pools, the playdates, the grocery shopping, the toilet paper restocking, the dishwasher loading, the dog food buying—I did (and still often do) most of the shit. When I was felled on that mountain, we'd been married for thirteen years, and for thirteen years, this was simply how it had been. I had a more flexible work schedule, so there's that, but also, I was better organized, and I could multitask, which he could not, so when it came down to it, I kept the household running.

Also, to be fair, this aspect of marriage, of parenthood, plays exactly into the baser parts of my personality. If I were to qualify my faults, my independence would probably rank number one, followed by a very close runner-up: my stubbornness. (My middle initial is "S," and growing up, my dad semi-joked that it stood for "stubborn.") This isn't a humblebrag, a false flag like you might cite on a college application. *"What's your greatest fault?" "Oh, I am just such a perfectionist! I always do my best and never cut myself a break."* No, I mean this seriously. I am too independent in ways that mean that I abhor asking for help, that I am loath to rely on others even when I really need to; and sometimes, I nearly drown rather than outstretch my arm and grasp a willing hand. Certainly, this is true in my marriage. Though I have often wished that Adam stepped up around the house, it was easy to fall on my saintly sword, to get wrapped up in my scorekeeping of how much I did in comparison to him, and to sink into my resentment of how much more capable (and tired) this made me.

Sometimes, Adam would say: "Just tell me what to do, and I'll do it!"

And I'd retort: "I don't want to have to *tell* you. No one tells me what to do. I just figure it out and get it done!"

And naturally, this type of argument wouldn't solve anything. He'd have no further clues as to how he could relieve me of the bulk of the household burdens, and I'd be no less irritated that he hadn't conjured up solutions on his own. If I asked him, he'd step up to the task, but the crux of the problem was that I didn't want to have to ask, and with me always handling everything anyway, he never had to take the initiative on his own.

In the deepest corners of my subconscious, which perfectly complemented my independence streak, I'd wonder: If I weren't here, would everything totally fall apart without me?

Once radiology had the X-rays, they paged the surgeon, and ushered him in as soon as he arrived at the ER. That's when I understood that I wasn't being overdramatic, shrieking like a lunatic as I lay splayed on the bunny hill. In firm but kind tones, the doctor explained that I needed surgery immediately, that mine was a critical, devastating injury. "I want to be clear," he said. "This is invasive surgery; this is not some easy fix, this isn't something we can just repair laproscopically. We won't know the full extent of the damage until we get in there."

Adam pressed him on the best-case scenario. The best case was six weeks non–weight bearing. (To the never injured, this means absolutely no weight on your foot or limb.) The worst case was . . . longer. Months maybe.

I was high as could be by then on my glorious IV drip, but sober enough to turn to Adam (again) and ask: "How are we going to manage?"

As the doctor ran through what was to come in the next few hours, I couldn't bear to listen. Instead, I focused on what would come once we arrived back in Los Angeles. My physical recovery seemed secondary to maintaining the seamlessness of my family's schedule. Who could get the kids to the bus at seven fifteen a.m., since my husband was in his office by six a.m. each day? Who could deal with the dogs, two rambunctious Labradors who relied on my companionship and long walks? Who could prepare dinner? Who would drive to tennis practices and softball games and sleepovers?

"We'll figure it out," Adam said once the doctor left and the nurses returned to monitor my pain and to prep me for the OR. I nodded in agreement because what was the alternative? That we wouldn't figure it out? But nowhere in any of my Vicodin-infused cells did I believe him. Not even a tiny bit.

The nurses wheeled me off to surgery, and the very last thing I remember, as they had me count backward from ten (or one hundred?), was one of them leaning over, right close to my ear, and saying, "Don't worry, you're in good hands. We're going to take good care of you."

． ． ．

I woke up after the surgery with my leg wrapped and bandaged beyond recognition, with tubes coming out of various limbs, with my mouth sandpaper dry and my mind flighty and confused. Adam was sitting in the corner, hovering over his phone. He saw that I was awake and tried to assuage me, tried to be calm. The doctor joined us and delivered the diagnosis, which was worse than initially anticipated: the operation had required two bone grafts (donor bone from cadavers) to fill the chunk I'd obliterated (it was in a "million pieces," he said, "there was none of your original bone to put back together"); they'd inserted a titanium rod, a dozen or so screws. I wouldn't walk for *three months*, optimistically. *Non–weight bearing completely. Not even a toe touch.* I couldn't drive. I couldn't navigate the steps in our house. I couldn't even shower on my own initially. I was sent back to California with a machine designed to train my leg to regain its range of motion: I would sit in it for six hours a day, as it taught my joint how to bend again. When I wasn't sitting in the machine, I would be at physical therapy or confined to bed rest. My leg muscles would atrophy, and eventually, my right thigh would shrink so much that it would be closer in size to my bicep. (At one point, I could form a ring with both hands and more or less fit it around my thigh's circumference.)

I absorbed the news with the stoicism I developed over years of being a mother and the years prior to that when I flouted my independence like a Girl Scout badge upon my chest. I was too medicated to cry, too shell-shocked to do much more than press my pain button and beg the nurse (on day three of the hospital stay) to please just bring me the bedpan because making it to the restroom required too much strength, and I was already using up all of my strength on staying stoic.

Because I was bored and because my brain was pooling with (glorious) white noise from my pain pump, I posted about my accident on Facebook. An image of me before surgery, with tubes up my nostrils, and a snapshot of my leg, wrapped and swollen and unrecognizable, the morning after surgery. And something unexpected happened: a deluge not just of sympathy or frowny faces, but friends both near and far chiming in, texting me, texting my husband, imploring for ways that they could help. I hadn't asked for it; in fact, I'd probably have pushed it aside, brushed it off saying I was entirely okay, but there they were, reaching out through my hospital chamber saying: *Please, let us do something.*

Maybe this outpouring of support isn't unexpected to some. Maybe, simply because I prefer my own company to most group outings, or because I hate calling in a favor when

I need one, as I never want to put anyone out or because I have always gravitated to a small but tight-knit group of friendships rather than a wider-spread social network, it felt unexpected to *me*. But it happened, and it punctured a hole in the armor around my exterior, cutting through even the thickest part of my medically induced haze.

I wrote each person back, thanking them sincerely and with gratitude that couldn't be conveyed in an electronic reply but was pulsing through me nevertheless. Yet I was still unsure if I would take my friends up on their kind offers, not certain that I was ready to acknowledge that I couldn't shoulder the weight of this burden and recovery all on my own.

The first thing to assess when you can no longer walk is logistics. In your day to day, you don't consider stairs, you don't consider carrying a glass of water while balancing on crutches, you don't consider what a pain in the ass it is to leave your computer charger in the kitchen when your laptop is hovering at 7 percent and is your only connection to the outside world.

Initially, we thought we'd order a medical bed to place in my first-floor office, but there's no bathroom nearby, and at the very least, I wanted the autonomy of getting myself to the bathroom on my own. (Attempting to regain that last shred of dignity I'd abandoned with the nurse and bedpan.) Instead, I settled on a couch in our upstairs den, a mostly unused room that is tranquil and restorative except when my kids decide to use the TV to play Madden on the Xbox. The room has a small fridge, which meant that I could extend my crutch from the couch and almost weasel open the door, so I wasn't constantly calling out for help (I could slide off the couch and scoot over to the fridge on my butt if needed), and also a nice countertop, where I could store all of my meds, including the needles for the daily injections I had to give myself into my thigh so I didn't die of a postsurgical blood clot.

Once your immediate logistics are sorted, you think about what you take for granted like having two healthy adults in a household. I'd never considered how fortunate my family had always been for having not just me, but *us*. What an amazing luxury it was: two adults, both healthy, both present. And then, despite being one man (woman) down, another luxury, another gift came our way: an army that I didn't even know was behind me, an army that I didn't even know I could need.

The fucking cavalry showed up.

By the time we returned home from Colorado, a friend had already set up a dinner train: meals for my family were taken care of for the first month of my recovery. Moms who I didn't even know all that well, having only lived in Los

Angeles for two years, had signed up to pitch in, drop off a plate of homemade enchiladas, send delivery from a nearby Italian joint. A writer with whom I was friendly but not close sent me daily emails to check in on my progress and also an incredible bouquet of flowers that sat next to my needles and meds. Parents at our school bus stop offered to drop my kids off each afternoon. Another friend showed up three weeks in, when I literally hadn't left the house since my return except for PT, and helped me into her car and whisked me and my flaccid, atrophying leg out for a pedicure. Friends from afar sent me care packages of books and food, others stopped by to restock our fridge. There was a rotating circuit of women all week: I'd leave our front door unlocked, and they'd let themselves in, come and sit with me for a few minutes to break my doldrums, to cut through my acute boredom. (I was too medicated to focus on reading, and I'd already burned through anything interesting on Netflix.)

My father moved in with us for a few weeks to monitor my recovery. A nurse from the hospital in Colorado texted every few days to assess my progress and answer any questions. The rabbi at our synagogue, whom I'd never met personally and where I was nearly always a no-show, called and made me weep with appreciation when I hung up, simply at the realization that there were people out there who cared enough to be compassionate even without knowing me. A mom friend stopped by one afternoon after a particularly brutal doctor's appointment, in which I was told that my recovery was progressing well enough but certainly not quickly and that weight bearing was still far out of reach, and my friend simply sat with me in silence while I came completely undone with tears.

At the time of the accident, I was two and a half months away from my twentieth college reunion. I'd been an active alumna and felt deeply tied to my college days—if I heard certain songs on the radio (anything by Pearl Jam), I could lose myself to a nostalgic haze where it felt like no time had passed between then and now. So I was devastated when the doctors told me it was unlikely I'd be able to attend. I certainly wouldn't be walking by then, much less flying across the country on my own. I begged them for good news: *Please tell me that I could at least touch maybe a toe down, that perhaps I could be 10 percent weight bearing*, not just because I needed to cling to the optimism of making my reunion, but also because weight bearing meant some sort of return to normal life. The medical professionals would promise nothing. But my friends promised everything. They posted on Facebook to keep up my spirits, they emailed privately to buoy my recovery and the hope that I would make it back to Philadelphia for the weekend. They were with me in every (metaphorical) step of my rehabilitation in profound ways that I will never truly be able to forget or repay. One day at physical therapy, my PT stretched my leg to agonizing lengths (which in this situation meant bending it approximately twenty or so degrees) and marveled at my progress. He told me that his optimistic patients heal more quickly, that there was real science behind this: that perhaps the body produced fewer stress hormones or just perhaps the positive patients worked harder at their rehab. I grimaced at the pain he was inflicting but mostly thought of my friends, of my army, who were shouldering me through.

My children learned to be both autonomous and empathetic. They ran up the steps each afternoon after school to check on me; my daughter set up her karaoke machine by my couch to keep me entertained while I eased myself to the floor to embark on my slow, cruel, and mandated PT exercises. My son dutifully fetched my laptop charger or a spare fork or a bottle of water when asked, never whining like he would have in the past. My kids no longer had the luxury of me setting out their school uniform each night or packing their lunches or ensuring that homework was filed. So they learned to do it themselves, and in a surprise perhaps only to me, their martyr mother, everyone was all the better for it.

And my husband. My husband! The man who previously had to be told what to do, when to do it, how to do it, and sometimes why, too. This is what my husband did when I went down on that mountain: he pulled my family and me back up. He was the one who filled those backpacks, he was the one who signed the permission slips and reordered the dog food and, when the dinner train ended, cooked for our children, too. He raced home from work in the middle of the day three times a week to drive me to PT, though I told him I could slide down the stairs on my butt and then crutch to an Uber (a terrible idea, as I fell on my crutches trying to navigate a step in our kitchen at five weeks and nearly set my recovery back to zero). In the early days, he carried me into the shower, where I would sit in a chair and let the hot water relieve my broken body, and then he would retrieve me and carry me out. He did all of this without complaint, because, as he said to me once, simply, "After all the years that you did so much, it was my time to show up."

So we didn't go to Mexico for our thirteenth anniversary, and instead on that day when we had married and avowed ourselves for better or worse, my husband dropped everything at his office in the middle of the day, helped me down the steps and eased me into the passenger seat of his car, and took me to physical therapy. This is the metaphor. Sometimes—many times—both in life and in marriage, you hope for the sunset overlooking the ocean off a deserted beach in the Mayan Riviera, but what you get is a drive to physical therapy. That's okay. Maybe it's actually how it should be.

I didn't realize I had an army—my husband, my children, my friends in a relatively new city, my parents, a nurse, a rabbi, my college acquaintances who came to mean more to me than I could have known when I was twenty-one—until I needed that cavalry, and they were there to have my back. I was forty-one, and I was still independent in ways that had defined me since childhood. I was still stubborn in ways that gave me the endurance to crutch around my neighborhood block at six weeks into my recovery, even though it took me seventeen minutes. But independence and self-preservation can only go so far, even in your fifth decade in life, even when you think that you have things pretty well figured out.

Three days before my college reunion, my doctor gave me clearance for 10 percent weight bearing. This meant I could touch my toe down, albeit delicately; this also meant that I embraced my independent streak and made it to Philadelphia for my reunion, though Adam offered to accompany me for safety. (I said, *No, I can do this myself.*) A few weeks after that, I transitioned off my crutches to a cane, and then, eventually, I was back on my own two feet. Standing on my own, but also standing on the shoulders of my army.

Eventually, I returned to the grocery shopping and the bus pickups and the carpooling. I made dinners again for my family; I organized everyone and hustled them out the door. But something profound had shifted in our household: appreciation for one another, appreciation for our health. The knowledge that though Adam didn't always pick up the slack, he could, and he did, and that made all the difference.

When the mountain broke me in two, he, and everyone else, helped piece me back together.

It's funny, to be at midlife and recognize that as well as you know yourself, there are still lessons to be learned. That for all of your years of experience, you still need to leave room to be malleable, to be surprised, to allow life to take you to unexpected places. Like how you cope when you cannot walk for three months. Like how those around you cope as well, and how they prove themselves to be more worthy than you realized, even when you already found them worthy enough.

Now, after all of this, I give people more benefit of the doubt. I am quicker to offer help if I sense that a friend is in need. I am quicker to ask for help if I am the one needing. Though I already considered myself empathetic, I find myself more caring, more open, even more charitable. No one can do anything in this world without the aid of others.

It's been two years now, and what matters, when I think back on all of this, is not that I shattered my leg, that it aches when the clouds roll in, that I'll never run that marathon, that I will always have a five-inch scar spanning from my knee to my shin, or that some days, I limp like I am eighty-three, not forty-three. What matters is that when I went down on that mountain, there were so many others there to help me back up, and that in doing so, they shifted more than just my literal balance.

I worried that my injury would upend everything. It turns out that it did.

10

The Breathtaking Potential of the Attosecond

JESSICA LAHEY

Time may be the most commonly used noun in the English language, but for most of my career, it was a precious, fleeting, ever-waning resource. I am a teacher, one of those lucky souls who knew, from the moment I stood in front of my own classroom, that the die was cast. I was twenty-eight, and I could see an entire career stretched out in front of me.

For much of my first year as a high school English teacher, I struggled to stay twenty-four hours ahead of my students. I slept little, I ate as I worked, and I hardly saw my husband. I felt time's scarcity at the close of every day. I was forever in need of a little more, just five minutes before the bell, a few extra classes before vacation starts. There was always one more thing to cover, thousands of facts to teach, skills to master, and competencies to meet during each school year, and never, *ever* enough time for it all.

Through my thirties and early forties, I continued to learn and grow as a teacher, and while the workload never diminished, I became more efficient. I learned to ignore the nitpicky, time-sucking details of the job and focus instead on the big picture: teaching middle school kids how to be curious, competent, and educated adults. Given that lofty mandate, the aesthetic perfection of my bulletin boards and my plans for elaborate, color-coded grading schemes just did not warrant any of those precious minutes in my day.

Time, after all, is a specious construct in education; the units that govern a teacher's day are an administrative fabrication. A school "hour" measures only fifty minutes, mortared together between wasteful, messy layers of students settling in and shuffling out. A teacher's day contains eight of these alleged hours, and, as we are constantly reminded by our grade books and school calendars, a presumptive year is really the span of 180 days, minus five to ten for mandatory state testing and three or four reserved for assemblies.

The meticulous planning of August always gives way to survival mode by November, and come June's final reckoning, the math never, ever checked out. Things got lost. Important things.

I lost time with my students to talk, to commiserate. I lost the opportunity to express my sympathy over the death of Squeaky, Liesel's beloved guinea pig. I lost lunch with Kevin, who just might be sliding into depression. I lost evening phone calls to touch base with parents who need to hear something—anything—positive about their kid.

I mourned these losses, of course, but educational exigence trumped emotional exorbitance.

And then, in my late forties, I began teaching in an inpatient drug and alcohol rehab for adolescents. That's when a writer named Alan Burdick and a student I'll call Alexa taught me a little something about how time *really* works.

I read Burdick's book *Why Time Flies: A Mostly Scientific Investigation* while on the road at a teaching conference. Thanks to Burdick, I discovered time can accommodate more than I figured. We don't live *in* time, he explains, we dictate our participation in it. We can schedule and calculate and allot time, but our emotions have the final say over its ebb and flow.

Time flies, races, or crawls depending on our emotional state. The more charged our feelings, the more our perception of time slows, and when these emotionally charged moments are happening with a person we care about or can identify with, time slows even further.

The more I know my students, the more time I can give them. Empathy, it seems, has the power to slow the passage of time and make the calculus of my teaching life work. Knowledge of and empathy for my students are not disposable remainders; they are the most important factors in my professional equation.

> We bend time to make time with one another, and the many temporal distortions we experience are indicators of empathy; the better able I am to envisage myself in your body and your state of mind, and you in mine, the better we can each recognize a threat, an ally, a friend, or someone in need. But empathy is a fairly sophisticated trait, a mark of emotional adulthood; it takes learning and time.

Burdick's analysis makes a lot of sense to me (and I particularly enjoy the implication that I am, at long last, an emotional adult). Emotional maturity has its benefits: the longer I teach, the more I understand about my students. The more I understand my students, the more I can empathize with them. The more I can empathize, the more time I have to give them.

This is when Alexa entered my classroom and smacked me in the face with the reality of my precious, pretty syllogism.

Alexa had arrived the day before, fresh off a rough detox. She'd been taking a bit of everything on the substance abuse menu—pain pills when she could afford them, heroin when she could not, weed and booze to round things out.

Alexa had no interest in my class, or in talking to me at all, really. She was quiet in the first week, biding her time until my second class to unleash the full firepower of her emotional arsenal on me and my well-laid lesson plans.

The writing assignment that day was based on the first section of Stephen King's *On Writing*, a simple and straightforward prompt: write about a snapshot memory from your childhood, like King's memory of carrying a cinder block across the garage while pretending to be a strong man in the circus. No backstory, no grand metaphors or lengthy narrative arc—just a snapshot, in a paragraph or two.

I passed around some lined paper and freshly sharpened pencils, praying someone—anyone—would cooperate and write. Teacher muscle memory kicked in as I quieted the jokesters, encouraged the anxious, and repeated my instructions to the inattentive hyperactive. Support, encourage, redirect, repeat. Support, encourage, redirect, repeat.

I joked around with the two counselors in the back of the room as I waited for the kids to focus.

At least one counselor attends my class, in case one of the students has to use the bathroom (they must be accompanied) or if behavior issues arise.

As I walked back up to the front of the classroom, most of the students turned their attention to the paper in front of them, and a few actually started to write. One boy in the back who I'd been told was reeling from a hairy opiate detox stared out the window. I turned my attention to Alexa, who had pushed her paper and pencil away, closed her eyes, rested her head on folded arms, and clearly intended to go to sleep.

Deep breath, remember to support, encourage, and redirect.

Support.

"Alexa, do you need any help with the assignment?"

No response.

"Alexa, did you understand what I wanted you to write?"

Still no response, but after a beat, she opened her eyes

to meet mine. Message delivered: she had no intention of writing.

Encourage.

"Do you want me to sit down with you and talk through a topic?"

No, her eyes said, she did not.

"Do you have any ideas?"

You betcha, plenty of ideas, her eyes replied as she reached for her black, three-ring treatment binder.

"I have to do my timeline, so I'll just finish that," she said as she extricated her "drug timeline," a wavy, black-markered line drawn across three pieces of taped-together copy paper. It's a rehab-mandated chronicle of her drug and alcohol abuse that begins at one end of the page with her first drink, details all the smokes and injections and pills and injections along the way, and arrives at the other end of the line with the drug-induced train wreck that landed her in my rehab classroom.

Redirect.

"No, we are not doing treatment work right now. It's school-time, so I'd love it if you'd work on this essay for me."

She scowled.

"Well, *I'm* doing treatment work right now, so I can't work on your fucking essay."

I lost it so fast, I'm not even sure what happened. I don't know if it was her words, her body language, the fact that she was making me look like an ineffectual ass in front of the counselors and my new boss, or some combination of the three, but I accelerated from supportive to pissed off in a flash.

Neural impulses travel through our body at a top speed of 250 miles per hour, so it took me about three one-hundredths of a second to register her rebellion, process the meaning of her words, register her intent, rise to anger, raise my arm toward the adolescent unit, point my finger, and say,

"Out. Get out of my classroom."

No one breathed, no one moved, save my trembling pointer finger.

In *Why Time Flies* I learned that scientists just recently broke what was called "the femtosecond barrier," the shortest increment of time humans can record, with a laser pulse half that long, or 650 attoseconds. Burdick writes, "The attosecond (10^{-18} second) has long existed as a theoretical entity but this was the first time anyone had actually encountered it. It's a newfound slice of time—a tiny one but with gargantuan potential."

Scientists may have only recently experienced the attosecond, but teachers have long been aware of its breathtaking potential.

That heartbreakingly short interval between before and after is all it takes to demolish a student-teacher relationship. Alexa was my student for another two months, but I never really got to know her. I never found out where she came from, what she hoped for, or what she'd experienced along the way; I squandered that opportunity. When I got angry, I lost the ability to empathize with her, to make time for her. Worse, I showed her I was just like every other adult in her life who had given up on her potential and sent her off to be someone else's problem, and I lost her—and the opportunity to teach her—forever.

Kids use drugs to take away untreated emotional and physical pain. When my students write about their earliest memories, they recount sexual abuse, emotional neglect, household substance abuse, abandonment, domestic violence, divorce, or parental incarceration. That first drink, smoke, or snort offered a welcome numbing: an opportunity to not feel and an escape from the pain. It's not just easier to stay numb than to hurt, it's a matter of survival. Many of my students have told me that without their drug of choice, a chemical escape hatch to oblivion, they would have killed themselves long ago.

However overwhelming, my students' childhood traumas are easy to quantify. The Centers for Disease Control and Prevention (CDC), in partnership with Kaiser Permanente, surveyed more than seventeen thousand patients about their childhood experiences, adult behaviors, and health status and found that the adverse childhood experiences (ACEs) lead to poorer health outcomes. ACEs are "dose-dependent," in that the more adverse childhood experiences a person has, the worse their health will be in adulthood.

The CDC developed a one-page quiz to measure this dose. The more trauma a person has experienced in childhood, the higher their ACE score. The higher the ACE score, the more likely that person is to suffer from poor health (depression, heart disease, lung disease, diabetes, stroke, cancer, severe obesity) and high-risk behaviors (smoking, drug and alcohol abuse, promiscuity, poor eating habits) in adulthood.

The interplay of ACEs and health isn't a simple equation, however, and that quiz score represents so much more than a 1:1 relationship between childhood physical abuse and death at age forty-five from cancer. The route from a violent childhood to early death takes a meandering, if predictable, path.

Adverse childhood experiences take a serious toll on a

child's neurological development. Their rapidly developing brains are affected on a cellular level by the pain and hurt they experience in their homes. Impaired or retarded brain development leads to impaired social, emotional, and cognitive development. Kids whose bodies and hearts have been hurt simply don't cope well with stress, don't learn how to relate to other people in healthy ways, and don't learn as well as a child who was fortunate enough to be born into a family of love and calm and consistency. Once a child's coping mechanisms get screwed up and they can't relate or bond with other people, they begin to take on risky behaviors that lead to more social problems, and the chasm continues to widen between "troubled kids" and their emotionally and cognitively healthy peers. The troubled kids grow into troubled adults, and the consequences of all that impairment, poor choices, risk taking, and maladaptive behaviors result in physical disease, disability, chronic mental health problems, and, finally, early death.

I've led my students through the CDC's Adverse Childhood Experience Questionnaire. It's not long; by the clock, it takes about ten minutes. I read each question out loud, then listen to their pencils scratch out answers, and I could swear it takes double that amount of time. It's intense, watching them reflect on their lives and fill in the blanks with their pain.

1. Did a parent or other adult in the household often . . .

   Swear at you, insult you, put you down, or humiliate you?

   or

   Act in a way that made you afraid that you might be physically hurt?

   Yes   No

   If yes enter 1 _____

   And, later in the questionnaire,

7. Was your mother or stepmother:

   Often pushed, grabbed, slapped, or had something thrown at her?

   or

   Sometimes or often kicked, bitten, hit with a fist, or hit with something hard?

   or

   Ever repeatedly hit over at least a few minutes or threatened with a gun or knife?

   Yes   No

   If yes enter 1 _____

It feels odd to grant points in exchange for instances of childhood terror, akin to administering the worst *Seventeen* magazine quiz ever invented, but with each question, each point accrued, I learn about the longest and most traumatic moments of my students' young lives and gain insight into their need to self-sabotage, hit, yell, and flee.

I meet my students in their first days of sobriety, when their chemical escape hatch has been shut off, and they have no other option but to feel the full weight of their accumulated pain.

Their emotions, long denied and dulled, reawaken with a vengeance, ready to wreak havoc. They can take up a lot of space and oxygen in my already cramped classroom, but thanks to experiences with students like Alexa, I have learned that when I let empathy in, time and space can expand to accommodate both my need to maintain control *and* their need to be heard. I learned that my easy power and privilege can grate up against their disadvantage and impotence.

I failed Alexa three years and a couple of hundred students ago, and in that time, I've learned how to capitalize on the vast promise contained in the shortest intervals, even when those moments are filled with anger, venom, and rebellion. If I'm present enough, and empathetic enough, an attosecond can expand to contain multitudes, to encompass their painful past and shape our possible future together.

A few months ago, Kyle (not his real name) arrived at rehab straight from juvenile detention, full of anger, hate, and sadness. His parents were alive, but in and out of jail, so he'd been bounced from one group home to another his entire young life, and he'd learned not to unpack his bag. He was quiet, but seething. He shuffled to his seat on the boys' side of the room with heavy, untied sneakers, dragged his folding chair out from under one of the tables, and sat down with a combination of a sigh and a groan. He folded his arms over his chest and looked out the window as the rest of the students sat down.

At some point during our first class together, we were going to have a pivotal now, that critical, deciding attosecond that would shape our future. I was going to have to get it just right or lose him, and the only way to get it right was by understanding him.

His appearance told some of his story, enough to get me started, anyway. He'd cut his own hair or let someone who was *seriously* high do it for him, as there were short patches randomly interspersed between longer sections in the back. His jeans were frayed at the knee and ankle and were much too big at the waist. Not in a relaxed-fit kind of way, but in a way that implied hand-me-down or thrift store. The rubber on the toes of his sneakers was worn down to the stitching, and the laces were frayed at the ends. He probably came to rehab carrying everything he owned in one small duffel.

I walked over to him and introduced myself.

"Hi, I'm your teacher, Jess. First order of business in my classroom is this: Do you have a book to read?"

"I don't read," he said, still looking out the window.

I paused, waiting for him to look at me. When he didn't, I squatted, so our faces were at about the same height. I was dying to fill up the uncomfortable air around us with words, but I didn't.

I waited, silent, longer than felt comfortable.

He turned to look at me.

"I mean, I *can* read. I just don't," he said.

"Well, let's start with this: Do you like made-up stories or real stories?"

"Neither," he replied, and turned back to the window.

I stood up and gave him some space. I'd try again later, as choosing just the right book for just the right person is my superpower.

The lesson that day was about perspective. We talked about first and third person, how one person's perspective on an event may differ wildly from another's. I read them two articles from a local paper, one from the perspective of a man who felt it was his right to demolish beaver dams in order to restore the landscape near his home to its natural state, and a letter to the editor in response to that article, written from the perspective of the beaver. Once the kids stopped laughing about the image of a beaver penning a letter to the editor, they agreed that the beaver had a valid point about ownership of land and what constitutes the "natural state" of a landscape.

At the end of this discussion, I asked the students to write two descriptions of themselves, one from their own perspective, and one from the perspective of someone else. That person could be anyone—a sibling, a neighbor, a counselor, a teacher.

After some hemming and hawing, everyone got down to work. Everyone but Kyle.

Kyle continued to stare out the window. I walked over to his desk, squatted down, and asked,

"Kyle, how about you get started writing? I'd love to read what you have to say."

"I don't want to," he replied.

Support.

"Start with whichever one is easier, then. Which one of the two descriptions do you think you could write?" I asked.

"Well, I could write the one from my perspective but not the other one," he said.

Encourage.

"Okay. Get started on the one from your perspective, and then we'll talk about the other one. How's that?" I said.

"Maybe later," he replied.

Redirect.

"Here. Here's some paper, and a pencil. Take a minute to think and then go ahead and get started."

Ten minutes later, he had scrawled a few sentences on the paper I'd given him, and had pushed the paper away to indicate he was done.

"Go ahead and try the other one now, the one from someone else's perspective," I said, pushing the momentum of his three lines of penciled text forward with my most confident and optimistic tone.

"I can't write that one," he said.

"Why not?" I asked.

"Because people don't think anything about me. People think I'm going to keep being an addict and go to prison just like all the other men in my family. That's all they think. Don't need to write that," he said, turning to face me, color rising out of his collar and into his face.

I did some mental ACE score math, adding the incarceration to his total, and squatted down again, even as I checked on the location of the counselor in the back of the room.

"Did any of those other men have a chance to go to rehab and start over?" I asked.

"No," he said, and drew a long breath in through his nose.

"Well," I said, "I guess you have something up on all of them, then. Why don't you write about the person they *could* see in a few months, when you leave here?" I suggested, and left to answer another students' question before he could reply.

Ten minutes later, as I made my way back up to the front of the room, I noticed Kyle was turned toward the wall to disguise the fact that he was writing on the tabletop. He'd drawn a huge heart with an arrow through it, the word "PAIN" drawn in all caps in the center with a Sharpie. He saw me looking, his shoulders tensed, hands curled into fists, and our now arrived.

He was there, yes, as was I, but so was Alexa and every student I'd left behind, and time seemed to stretch on and on to accommodate us all.

"Come on. I'll show you where we keep the cleaner and the paper towels, and then I'll help you finish that essay," I said.

We spent three long months together before he left for a sober living facility. Kyle's odd, jagged haircut grew out and was cut again, this time by someone with some sense and a professional license. I learned more about what landed Kyle in rehab, and he learned that I, too, am an alcoholic.

Recently I was playing the "guess my age" game with some of my students, and after I'd (correctly) guessed theirs, I challenged them to guess mine. Most underestimated my age, not because I look particularly young, but because from their thirteen-to-seventeen-year-old perspective, forty-seven is old-lady territory.

While I don't feel old, I do feel experienced. I never did convince Kyle to write that second essay about how others perceive him, but given some luck, sufficient health care, a therapist, and a few teachers willing to look past his attitude and recognize his pain, he'll have plenty of time left in his young life to find his voice, and tell that story.

The thing I've given myself permission to do now that I am forty is . . .

"Go to bed early. Arianna Huffington was not wrong. Sleep is like Wonder Woman serum."

—Veronica Chambers

"The thing I gave myself permission to do now that I'm forty is say no. Nope. Can't do it. No apologies, that's just the way it is. That's the other thing, I guess—I don't apologize much anymore."

—KJ Dell'Antonia

"To cut loose negative people from my life. No more lunching with downer dames. Life is short."

—Lee Woodruff

"Find more ways to have the people I love in my life, even if it means traveling. I used to think it was enough to be in touch with faraway friends via Facebook, but it's not the same. I use to mourn this as an unfixable problem but somehow as I've gotten older, I've gotten bolder about not accepting things the way they are."

—Sophfronia Scott

"Wear my hair long. Accept that I'm never going to stop biting my nails. Wear sneakers as shoes."

—Kate Bolick

11

The People Who Got Me Here

JULIE KLAM

Turns out, the reason people say being a grown-up is hard is because it is. No matter how old you are you want someone to come take care of you when the shit hits the fan. Like, say, when you're about to go to jail. . . . A few years ago, when I was only forty-seven, I had this thing happen. I was out of checks, and so I paid my rent with a bank check. As you know, you can't see when a bank check clears, because the money is already out of your account, so you just have to assume the recipient has cashed it and all is well. Apparently, it wasn't. My moronic/evil landlord had opened the check in his car, lost it, forgot he ever got it, and decided to evict me.

Sadly, I have been through this type of thing before. Once, after I got divorced and my daughter and I were living alone in a one-bedroom apartment, someone knocked on my door at nine o'clock at night and handed us a thirty days' leave notice (the building had decided to go co-op and we were in the way).

When I got this latest eviction notice in the mail, I called the landlord, told his voice mail the story, and assumed it was taken care of (because I had paid, after all). Also, I was having so many other difficulties in my life, I didn't have the bandwidth for much follow-up; I needed to assume something—this—would sort itself out.

No such luck. Cut to a few weeks later when I found out that because I hadn't paid attention to that paper (other than recycling it), I had to go to jail. Well, not jail. But NYC housing court, which is not far from NYC criminal court, where busloads of waiting inmates come every day. I panicked. I called my aunt Mattie who lives in New York City—my first instinct was to call my mother who lives all the way in Vermont, but nine out of ten times she is out of range for her phone to work—and told her what happened.

"Just call the landlord, see what's going on." It sounded as if she were eating something crunchy.

"Mattie!"

"What?" she said, still not understanding I was heading up the river.

"PLEASE! FIX! THIS!" I pleaded. I was standing on Broadway, walking my dogs, my knees were shaking.

"Okay," she said, understanding. She asked for the landlord's number and the phone number on the form. I gave the numbers to her and told her to call me back soon.

Before you think, I'm not reading another word of this histrionic woman's story, let me explain and perhaps you'll give me a pass for this moment of hysteria.

I was in the middle of a very wrenching divorce, living alone with my daughter, who was really struggling. I was way overdue on a book, and if I could have just finished it, that would've fixed a lot of things (financially and with regard to feelings of inadequacy), but I couldn't because I was too anxious and was also trying to remain in a constant wine spritzer haze. So, you see the problem.

And this is why I regressed to the state of a child who wants to stomp her feet and have somebody—anybody—make things right. I'm responsible as shit, and also I lose my mind when I get overwhelmed. I call my mother and my aunt every morning. We talk about what we ate/are going to eat, we talk about politics, and if there's anything I'm struggling with, I tell them and they give me advice that I may or may not take.

Not long after we hung up, as the dogs and I reached my building, she called me back and said she had talked to a nice man at the court who said I should not have ignored that paper and must come down there, there being housing court, and that it was serious, like right now serious. She picked up her car from the lot on Second Avenue, picked me up, drove me to lower Manhattan (with my mother on speakerphone the whole trip piping in advice like yenta Charlie of *Charlie's Angels*). We parked, I went to the correct window, and the clerk basically told me that I was an idiot for ignoring the original notice. Guilty as charged. She gave me a court date for the following week.

In the meantime I went to the bank to find out what the fuckity fuck happened to the check. The very nice bank official looked it up, which for some reason was way more complicated than it should have been in this era of the computer. He had to call several places before he was able to find that the check had *not* been cashed. He gave me a copy of the original with the date I had purchased it, and I scanned it and sent it to my landlord. He still couldn't find any record of payment, so I had to pay thirty bucks to stop the check, BUT because it was a bank check, it takes ninety days for the money to be returned to me. My rent is New York City ridiculous, so I didn't have another month's rent sitting in my bank account. I would have to wait for three months to be able to pay it to them, THE RENT I'D PAID THEM ALREADY. Is your head exploding yet? Because mine was. I had done nothing wrong; in fact, it was my over-conscientiousness that led me to get the bank check to begin with, because my landlord charges one hundred dollars if your check arrives after the tenth of the month. (Aren't you glad you don't live in Manhattan?)

On the way home from the bank I called my mother and Mattie and got just what I needed: heaps of sympathy. My mother said things like, "I didn't raise you for this!" And Mattie said, "Poor lamb!" A week later, Mattie drove me back to Lower Manhattan to the world of courts, with my mom again on speakerphone all the way.

I should reiterate that I'm not usually quite this feeble, but I'd used up all of my bravery in the previous few months and I was running on fumes emotionally.

I grew up fairly sheltered. My family was secure. My dad was a financial planner who did very well, my mother was a very attentive stay-at-home mom (which we now know means she worked her ass off but got no credit). If I have any issue with anything my mother did, it was trying to make my life as easy as possible. Which means, I didn't get a lot of experience solving my own problems. She was Deus ex Momia.

When I got married, I guess I expected that my life would

go the way my mother's did: my husband would make the money; I would make the kids. (This, even though before we were married, I was a successful journalist and Emmy-nominated writer for two TV shows.) Whatever I expected was not what happened. My husband was a TV producer, and his jobs would come and go, leaving us with inconsistent financial stability. It was stressful and not the romantic picture of life and marriage I'd envisioned.

Ten months after we were married I got pregnant. He was working on a show for one of the most tyrannical bosses I had ever encountered. I so wish I could remember his name so I could find him on social media and troll him. Anyway, when I was seven months' pregnant, I was diagnosed with preeclampsia. It was terrifying and awful. (The day I found out was the day of the New York City blackout of 2003, so I was peeing into gallon jugs all night in the dark . . . and no AC!) When I was induced a couple of weeks later, I lay in the recovery room while my daughter was in the NICU and got a voice mail on my little flip phone. It was the insurance company saying that because I had delivered when I did, they suspected I had lied about being pregnant when I got the insurance (my baby was two months early), and they didn't think they should pay for any of it. My husband was home asleep, and I was alone in the hospital with my underweight little girl. There were a lot of complications with the delivery that caused me to be in not great shape, physically. To wit, I couldn't get up by myself, and one of my hands was swollen the size of a football, and, well, enduring eighteen hours of labor and a C-section doesn't leave you with a lot of physical emotional reserves. But as shitty as I felt, I had this little baby (actually I had a Polaroid picture of her, because I couldn't see her, and didn't get to actually hold her until twenty-two hours after she was born), and I knew that I was going to have to take care of her and let nothing ever hurt her. My husband may or may not have been able to help me, I just didn't know. But I knew I could count on me. I would take any work doing anything.

I went home, leaving her in the hospital, and immediately got to work. As soon as I was able, I pitched magazines. Later, I wrote a book proposal with my daughter crawling around my chair. My marriage pretty much began disintegrating around the time our daughter was born, but we didn't split up until she was eight years old. Still, I had gotten accustomed to being responsible for a lot because that's how my marriage worked. But through the divorce, I had the magic bullets of my aunt Mattie and my mother. At the moments when I was falling apart for a variety of reasons, like every time we met with the mediator or talked about parenting schedules or divorce in any way, I would call them, Mattie would rub my head and tell me it would be okay, that nothing that was going wrong was going to kill any of us. My mom would spew fury about the people who were making my life difficult, and somehow I would be able to get back into the ring and keep going.

It also happened that at the time my husband and I were splitting up, Mattie's husband of thirty-seven years told her he was in love with another woman, and they, too, were divorcing. So we had this parallel shittiness going on that mostly helped us buoy each other. If you have gone through any kind of divorce, except maybe if you are Kim Kardashian and you've only been married seventy-two days, you know it's terrible. If you are the one who wants it, it's terrible, if you are *not* the one who wants it, it's terrible, if it's a surprise, it's terrible, if it was a long time coming . . . you get the idea. Sharing or dividing kids, dogs, whatever you have jointly—even if it's debt—is the pits. And having someone you love experiencing it at the same time is very profound. It's not someone trying to recall the experience; they are right there now.

A year after my husband and I separated, I started dating someone, a man, Dan, who lived in Iowa. Things had gotten more serious, and he had recently moved to New York to be closer to me. but I needed my daughter to be okay with it, which was proving a little more difficult than I had hoped. She did not want me to date or get married. I really loved Dan, but I felt like I already appeared to be enough of a mess, my divorce was taking forever, my daughter wasn't on board, so the last thing I wanted to do was burden him with my dumb housing issues.

With my court date pending, I told him what had happened. He was very upset with me for not telling him about it sooner, he could have given me the extra money and all of this could have been avoided. He immediately wrote me a check for the amount that was past due because of the bank check mishap and I mailed it—certified—to my landlord. I felt like I'd been holding my breath for four years and I finally exhaled. I think sometimes we have no idea how much we are holding up while we are doing it, because if we became aware of it, we might fall into a puddle. But after, it was clear.

I had felt for a long time, early in my marriage and through the divorce, that I was alone, aside from my mother and Mattie comforting me and helping me take care of the chronic anxiety that has plagued me since childhood. Things that cause normal people to worry can give me a full-blown panic attack. I had to do everything myself, or it wouldn't get done. I mean I had to do these things myself. You can't ask your mother to stand in for you with the divorce mediator, she can't write a note to your publisher saying, "Please excuse my daughter's book lateness, she's having some mental issues." I also felt like if anyone helped me, it was another Deus ex Momia and it wouldn't "count." Or maybe it would disable my ability to do things for myself. Or I wouldn't get the gold star in the Book of Accomplishments. Dan was clear, though. We were helping each other in many ways. He could do this, and maybe the next thing, I could do for him.

Mattie drove me to my court date, and I felt more secure with both her and Dan behind me. I did have to keep telling her to be quiet because there are very strict rules in the judicial halls. Also she kept trying to sit in the seat that the court officer said no one was allowed to sit in. My scummy landlord sent a magnificently sleazy lawyer like you've never seen, slicked-back hair, a clip-on tie with a palm tree on it; the kind of guy who would happily jail his mother for not reading a street parking sign correctly. He had forgotten the files he needed, because his life goals involved wrecking other people's days at every turn, so we had to sit an extra hour waiting for his minion to bring the damning evidence against me. We watched person after person go through the process, a guy who had not paid his rent in a year, a woman who spoke only Spanish and had not understood her lease, a homeless man who was trying to work out a housing deal. And the judge was an absolute mensch. He took every case and slowly and methodically tried to figure out how the tenant could keep or find housing. He negotiated a cheaper apartment for a gentleman and got the landlord to lower the total of the back rent the guy owed (because he had cancer and was out of work). He asked another guy who hadn't paid rent for a year if there was anyone who could help him or if he had any way to get money. The guy said he was working on something, and though it sounded like bullshit to me, the judge granted him more time. He told the guy he really, really had to try.

The ambulance chaser the landlord sent finally got his papers, and we went up to the judge. I had a good feeling about it, mainly because my rent was paid up. I knew I wasn't going to be homeless, but there was another problem. If you rent your home in New York City, and you go to housing court for any reason, you are put on a blacklist whether you win or lose your case. And once you are on the blacklist, you have a really hard time renting again. Some people hire attorneys to get them off it, but it's not guaranteed to work, and it's expensive. It is terrible and unfair, and the existence of it forces many people to suffer under slumlords because reporting them will make it virtually impossible to move. (This is why I didn't sue the landlord two apartments ago when we didn't have gas for nine months.)

I told my story to the judge, he asked me why I had ignored the first notice, and I told him I was an idiot. He nodded, fixed it all, told me not to throw things away anymore. I thanked him and thanked him, and Mattie and I left and headed to lunch (at a place called the Clam, where we dined on lobster rolls and wine). On the way we had my mother on speakerphone. She was so happy I wasn't going to the clink and thanked Mattie for taking care of me.

I started to cry and Mattie put her hand on my leg. I know they thought I was crying from relief. And it was partly that, but I was also crying because it hit me that I was not going to have my mom and Mattie "taking care of" me forever. I mean, c'mon, I knew that getting to forty-seven with both parents and my dear aunt was unbelievably fucking lucky. The fact that they were healthy and clearheaded was something not to be taken for granted, and boy I do not. And one day, they won't be here. It is true I have other great supports, but nothing is like that. No one else feels that, like, legally I am their responsibility. And when the awful days do come, I don't know what I'll do. I reassure myself that I know them so well that I can imagine just what they'd say. According to my daughter, that's true. At least once a week she says, "God, you sound like Bubbe, only more shrill." Or, "Uh, thanks, Mattie!" It's not meant to be a compliment, but I take it as one.

I guess one of the things about getting older is we develop an appreciation for the team who got us here, whatever your support system is: friends, teachers, therapists, or family. And then of course we start to lose them. But if they've helped form you into who you are, then they never really leave you; they're always with you in whatever you do, and maybe that's the point.

12

Tried That, Doing Me

SUJEAN RIM

ON BEING 40(ISH)

TRIED THAT, DOING ME

ON BEING 40(ISH)

TRIED THAT, DOING ME

ON BEING 40(ISH)

TRIED THAT, DOING ME

ON BEING 40(ISH)

TRIED THAT, DOING ME 165

ON BEING 40(ISH)

TRIED THAT, DOING ME

ON BEING 40(ISH)

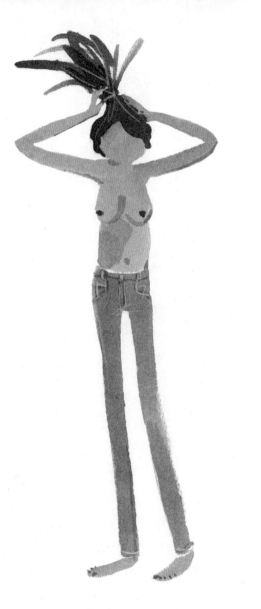

TRIED THAT, DOING ME

ON BEING 40(ISH)

ON BEING 40(ISH)

13

I Don't Have Time for This

SOPHFRONIA SCOTT

The woman who does not require validation from
anyone is the most feared individual on the planet.
—MOHADESA NAJUMI

A few days after the 2016 presidential election, my friend M calls. I'm happy she is calling, happy to see her name on my landline's caller ID and not the usual anonymous toll-free numbers announcing telemarketers. I pick up the phone with a sunny "Hi, M!"

The tone of her voice sounds low, hesitant, and gentle—the approach of someone speaking to the bereaved at a funeral. "How are you doing?" she asks. The word "Good!" bounces out of my mouth before I realize it's too upbeat.

"Really?"

"Yeah."

I know I'll have to start explaining because it's not as though she doesn't believe me. I think her "Really?" is more a question of "How?" as in, "How is it you aren't floored by this?" Most everyone in our circle is. I have friends who have seriously hit the deck, falling into deep depression, even getting physically ill, as a result of the news that we would have a reality show real estate entrepreneur with the hair of a Muppet as our next president.

It has been a week since the election, and the world—the liberal progressive world, or bubble, if you will—is still spinning with disbelief and despair: professors canceling classes, writers abandoning their writing, and mothers on social media lamenting that they don't know how to explain the election results to their daughters.

My friend has called me to commiserate. But I'm not miserable. I haven't given a thought to being miserable. The sun is pouring through the windows of my yellow kitchen, my family is healthy, my friend is on the phone, and I'm glad to hear her voice. So I will try to figure out how to gently put into words the overpowering feeling I have more and more as I walk through middle age:

I don't have time for this.

I don't have time to be miserable; I don't have time to take on the negative energy sweeping the country, energy that isn't mine, energy that would surely paralyze me if I let it in.

This doesn't mean I don't feel the same shock and disappointment that she and so many other people are feeling. It doesn't mean I don't respect her sadness. I recognize the hard and fantastical times that are surely before us. But I don't have time to be floored by it. There are other things on my mind like:

- Rehearsals, along with my twelve-year-old son, for a community production of *A Christmas Carol*. I'm playing the Ghost of Christmas Present. I've never done such a thing before, so I'm learning how to dance onstage while wearing a long dress and wielding a glitter-sprinkling wand.
- A Kickstarter campaign I'm overseeing to help fund the production.
- A writing workshop I'm teaching to undergraduates at a nearby university.
- An event I'm organizing at same university for a visiting writer.
- A virtual book tour I'm implementing for a friend's book.
- Getting the oil changed in my minivan.
- The book review I'm writing that's overdue.
- The Advent-related duties I have at my church, where I serve a leadership role.

A long list, yes, but let me clarify—I'm not saying I'm too busy to think about the results of the election. I'm saying I want to focus instead on the unique, amazing present moment of my life and drink every ounce of joy it offers—the wondrous faces of my students discussing their first essays; the crispness of the skin on a chicken I've managed to roast just right; my veteran actor son saying to his rookie mother after rehearsal, "Mama, you're doing great!" I savor these moments. They sit tart and bright and sweet on my tongue like the taste of hibiscus tea with honey. From these moments I can cultivate gratitude and from gratitude I distill grace. The grace allows me to walk through the world as a child of God—beloved and well cared for.

I don't easily give up these moments of grace and joy. At fifty-one I've experienced enough to know that when tragedy strikes, these moments evaporate with breathtaking speed in the bitter cold of loss, and I'm left grasping for them, my wounded spirit parched. That's what it was like when a gunman opened fire just down the hall from my son's third-grade classroom at Sandy Hook Elementary, killing twenty-six, including one of his best friends. My heart, shrunken with horror and grief, felt small and dry as though it would never feel joy again. The worst had happened, and the world shockingly, unbelievably rolled on. In my mind the world will continue rolling on, and the worst will happen again and will keep happening. What will I be doing in the meantime? Holding on as well as I can to what is positive and full of light and life because I know how easily it can be torn from my hands.

Recently I had a conversation with a white friend who felt a sincere need to delve deeply into the issue of race. He told me he'd been reading a lot and was in dialogue with a lot of different people about his views, experiences, and questions about how he could be a better ally. I applauded him for all this but his tone was, like M's, one of commiseration. There was a point where he shook his head and made a comment bemoaning the things I must have to deal with and suffer on a regular basis as a black woman. I knew he was saying this out of love and concern, but I managed to communicate to him that I don't linger in a mindset of suffering. If I did, I'd have to be in that frustrated, angry space *all the time* because racial issues abound (one of my brothers who lives in Florida had a slur spray-painted on his home), and our society is bewilderingly slow to understand as a whole why the Black Lives Matter movement is so necessary. But I feel that it is more important for me to be joyful in the world and to do my writing and focus on the positive over the negative.

A passage from the book *The Meaning of Michelle: 16 Writers on the Iconic First Lady and How Her Journey Inspires Our Own* speaks of this same feeling and of its importance. In her introduction Veronica Chambers, the book's editor, writes "[Michelle Obama] seems determined to remind us that—despite the challenges within and outside of our community—Blackness is not burdensome, and we, like all other human beings, have joy as a birthright, one we must work, sometimes daily, to claim."

It is work to claim this joy. It can make me something of an outsider and lead to awkward moments like the one on the phone with my friend. I don't watch the news or feel like I have to keep up on the latest binge-worthy television shows. Being such an outsider is worth it, though, because here's the amazing thing: when I focus, aided by the amazing crystal-clear lens that middle age provides, on what's good right now, life expands. Now it's easier (not easy, but easier) not to be thrown by unhelpful matters like the outcome of the election. Thus, my guiding philosophy when it comes to a lot of popular concerns: "I don't have time for this."

There's a video a friend posted in one of my Facebook feeds from the *Baroness von Sketch Show*. It's labeled "Welcome to your 40s. Welcome to not giving a shit at the gym."

In it, the gym's receptionist, upon learning a member has turned forty, escorts the woman to a different area of the locker room, an area populated solely by women over forty.

They're all naked.

They are women who have grown so comfortable with their bodies that they eschew the carefully placed towels and dainty footsteps of their earlier years. The younger women across the room look on them in complete fright and in fact, at the end of the video, one of the nude ladies even says, "Who wants to go to the sauna and scare the shit out of the twentysomethings?" The response? "Yeah!"

I laughed out loud at this video. I loved the joy, the sense of release these women so comically displayed. I want to continue living that kind of lightness and freedom. At this age it's easier to be bold, to push distraction aside or refuse to take it on when offered.

As one of the naked women in the gym observed, "The mental space freed up by not giving a shit? It's delicious." On any given day I may seem like a horse running the earth unbridled—that strong and that free. Sometimes there's a scent in the air so beautiful, earthly, and alive that it makes me feel ravenous, like this sharp awakening moment wants to cut me open to prove how empty I am, to show how much space there is for me to fill. What will I fill it with? I could eat the dirt and all that is in it and sense it wouldn't be enough. I am giddy. I want to fly.

It has taken me a long time to access such harmony. I was thirty-five and living in New York City on 9/11. I was a journalist and working on a novel. My words fell away then, so I have deep compassion for the ones who have stopped writing now. But those days of not writing turned into months when I suffered a miscarriage about ten weeks after the towers collapsed. My life wasn't what I wanted it to be—I'd always said I wanted to work for myself and write from home so I could raise children and not be on company hours. I started to change course but did it slowly—in my thirties I still thought I had all the time in the world. I managed to have a baby at thirty-eight and I published one novel, but then I spent too many years not thinking about my own writing, at least not prioritizing it. I was too engrossed in writing other people's books as part of my editing/ghostwriting business. Of course I was focused on making money—who isn't? Year after year I kept thinking I'd find the time to write my next novel, but it wasn't happening.

Then in 2011, right before my forty-fifth birthday, my sister Theo died. She'd been in ill health following bariatric surgery she'd had a few years earlier, but she was only forty-three. With my grief I felt a deep, deep shock: we aren't guaranteed our time here. It's not like I wasn't aware of this before. Six years earlier, on October 2, 2005, the playwright August Wilson died at the age of sixty. Less than four months later the playwright/author Wendy Wasserstein also died. She was only fifty-five. I'm a fan of both of these writers, and I think often about the depth and gravity of the work they'd left behind. The complete set of Wilson's Century Cycle plays, ten in all including *Fences*, *The Piano Lesson,* and, my favorite, *Two Trains Running*, stays in front of me on my desk, right next to my computer. I knew if I had the tiniest aspiration to produce that amount of work at that level, I had to get my butt in gear. But I was thirty-nine then and didn't act.

At forty-five, for me grieving my sister's death, time lost suddenly felt like precious water poured out on hard, dry soil. And I did act then. In 2011 I finally began to cut back on clients, and I went back to school to earn my MFA in creative writing. There was a lot of sacrifice and work involved in making a commitment to my dream—I even drove a school bus to earn money while I was in graduate school. I am fierce about my time and what gets my attention because less than two months after I began my MFA studies Whitney Houston died. In the back of my mind I see her haunted face from the 2009 interview she did with Oprah where they discussed Whitney's substance abuse issues. She acknowledged her singing had fallen by the wayside and said, "I wasn't remembering the gift that God had given me." The look on Whitney's face is heartbreaking. I never want to look like that. After she died I couldn't listen to her music. The sound of her divine, soaring voice pierced me with sadness. I mourned that voice, not because it was gone now, but because it was gone long before Whitney herself left this earth. When I think of the prospect of wasting my gift, I'm more apt to stand my ground—Kelleyanne Conway doesn't get to occupy my brain space.

Sometimes I remind myself of my aunt Rosie. My mother's older sister, age eighty-three, died recently. She was a prickly personality—I admit to being afraid of her sometimes. She had no filters and no problem telling you what's what. When I visited her not long after I married, she whispered to me, very seriously, "You know you can leave him if you're not happy with him, right?"

She wasn't joking. I nodded.

It wasn't until her funeral, as I heard her children and grandchildren talk about the wisdom she was constantly trying to impart—and how they often didn't listen, to their own detriment—that I realized what had made her so prickly all those years: she was impatient. She'd seen a lot, experienced a lot. This was a woman who earned her GED and started a career at the age of fifty. "Mentoring young women" was listed in her obituary among her interests, along with baking the homemade rolls she was known for. As she imparted wisdom, even in what she said to me about my marriage, I know she was thinking about time—she wanted to save us time. She wanted to not waste her own. But she saw her advice not taken. She saw her children make life-altering mistakes. It often made her bitter. I'm not an advice giver but I recognize the feeling of impatience. It comes from being all too familiar with the woes of the world, especially when history repeats and events happen again and again. If I'm not careful, I know bitterness could take root in me.

However, I will not cut myself off from the woes of the world. That's impossible, anyway, unless I become a hermit. Instead I prefer to cultivate, as Joseph Campbell writes in *The Power of Myth*, a "joyful participation in the sorrows of the world." He says, "All life is sorrowful; there is however an escape from sorrow; the escape is nirvana—which is a state of mind or consciousness, not a place somewhere, like heaven. It is right here, in the midst of the turmoil of life. It is the state you find when you are no longer driven to live by compelling desires, fears, and social commitments, when you have found your center of freedom and can act by choice out of that."

To me this means I don't care about certain things, but it also means I can care deeply about others. I care enough to know what and when to let go. It means when the hard stuff happens, I'm not inclined to move with the masses. I'm not going to reiterate what's already being said, post what's already being posted, join groups that are or will soon become echo chambers. I can step back so I can see more clearly the answer to the question I ask in times of difficulty: "What am I supposed to be doing?" There is work to be done and I'm seeking the work that I, because of personality, opportunity, or circumstance, am best suited to do. I'm seeking the answer most in line with who I am and what I believe.

That is how I, as a woman of this age, engage with the world. This is what I want to tell my friend on the phone. But I'm all too aware of the possibility that I could easily come off like a bull in a china shop. I don't want to break anything, especially not bonds or hearts. I don't want to scare anyone, not even the twentysomethings in the sauna.

I don't want to seem callous and uncaring. So how do I relate this? How do I invite my friend into this space, one she can inhabit, too, because she is older, by a few years, than I am. How do I share what I've come to learn?

These are the words I choose to say, ever so gently, to my friend: "The world was broken before the election. The world is broken now." But I've learned the strongest stance I can take is to hope and pray for its wholeness, and walk through the world in a way that shows I believe such wholeness is possible, no matter what else is going on. This is the best use of my time.

14

Youth Dew

LEE WOODRUFF

A few weeks before my mother's fortieth birthday, she shocked my sisters and me by doing two completely uncharacteristic things. The first was to accompany my father to a convention in New York City, leaving an ancient, lemon-faced stranger in charge of us at ages twelve, ten, and nine. We still discuss Mrs. Long's acerbity, the wobbly, pencil-eraser-size wart on her jawline, and our feelings of betrayal at my mother's decision to abandon us to someone so completely unfamiliar with children.

But it was the second thing, if you knew my mother, that was far more perplexing. She returned from that trip with hundreds of dollars of Estée Lauder makeup and skin care. Our mother had walked into a high-end, New York department store, let strangers touch her face, and then blown her weekly food budget on a self-indulgence!

The elegant robin's-egg blue boxes, with their neat gold trim, emerged from her luggage as unlikely as moon rocks, beautiful, but somehow ominous and strange. My sisters and I formed a crescent around our mother, captivated as she arranged each new item on the kidney-shaped dressing table: liquid foundation, powdered blush, and a bottle of "Youth Dew" perfume, complete with a posh gold bow. For weeks afterward, we snuck into our parents' bedroom to inhale the mystery of the fragranced lotions, run the sable brushes across our skin, and touch the pressed shadows, careful not to leave a mark.

This new, forty-year-old mother with a vanity of expensive cosmetics was confusing. She had always been pretty, in a natural, practical way, but she did not wear makeup, had never "put on her face" or owned a tube of mascara. Her one nod to beauty was a slash of red lipstick when she left the house, a vestigial female commandment from the 1950s.

In some ways, my mother was ahead of her time, eschewing alcohol and tobacco, avoiding the sun. She was an early devotee of yoga, long before Lululemon made it fashionable. She was also an introvert, prim and germ-phobic, famously confiding that on New Year's Eve, she hid in bathrooms at midnight to avoid kissing strangers.

So, what had come over our thrifty, no-nonsense mom, the religious recycler of aluminum foil, the homemaker who worked every nub of Ivory soap down to a sliver? Was this purchase simply an indulgent act or an outward clue of inner turbulence? I would never really know.

I envied my friends whose moms dished after school, weighing in on crushes and fashion, keeping abreast of the latest gossip, like early versions of the Gilmore Girls. My mother's interior landscape, her desires and disappointments, would remain largely a mystery to me. The first time I saw her cry was when she dropped me off at college.

"I can't believe I'm going to be forty," I recall her saying once. It was the only clue my teenaged self had that this milestone was disturbing. Yet, I have no distinct memories of my mother's actual birthday. True to her desire not to make a fuss, I cannot recall any special celebration, or anxious "over the hill" talk.

I tiptoed over the line from girlhood to adolescence during the tumult of the 1970s. Outside the ordered confines of our small, center hall colonial, messages swirled about feminism and equality, power and womanhood, beauty and aging. It was impossible not to hear them, not to be seduced by all those demands for change.

Viewed from the narrow vantage point of a teenager, my mother's life was one of circumscribed roles, devotion and duty, repetition and interiors. My father left the house each day and engaged with the greater world. He had a career and an income; he traveled to other cities and countries. That was what I wanted. And my mother encouraged me to want it.

"Always be able to take care of yourself," she had urged me. "Have a vocation." And I listened. She had gotten a master's degree in speech pathology, although she'd stopped working when I was born.

Her life had a pattern: a routine of errands, cleaning and food preparation, caring for her aging parents. She was home when my father returned from work, vegetables washed, the rice water measured, the chicken breasts, like two hands separated in prayer, already baking in the oven. I picture her reading in the living room, the late-afternoon light illuminating the dust flecks that danced in the air like atoms.

That mother was the polar opposite of the one I imagined

on the cusp of her fortieth birthday, walking confidently down Fifth Avenue, surrounded by hovering salesgirls at the Estée Lauder counter. And in the months following that trip, those feelings of independence and excitement must have been slowly extinguished. The beautiful creams and shadows remained largely untouched, as if she'd felt herself unworthy of such everyday luxury. Only the bottle of Youth Dew perfume was used with any regularity.

Decades later, I stood at the mirror over my bathroom vanity, surrounded by more lotions and creams than my mother could have imagined. My mouth involuntarily formed an O as I applied the last of my mascara and brushed out my hair. I added a swish of lip gloss, checked the overall effect, and headed downstairs to set out food for what we'd dubbed "the mother of all parties."

My husband, Bob, and I had many things to celebrate that night: the recent birth of our twin girls, an impending move to London, and my own fortieth birthday. Bob, a TV reporter, was being transferred overseas with ABC News to become a foreign correspondent. While this was his dream, I was up for the adventure. I'd been a willing partner in the three-legged race called marriage; moving frequently, working, single-parenting during his absences and nursing the pilot light of a writing career. Above all else, we were a team.

The cherry blossoms in our Washington, DC, backyard had long been scattered by a hard rain, but the azaleas at the perimeter blazed in red, white, pink, and orange. I'd spent days working on the appetizers and desserts, months collecting and washing glass jars to wrap thin wire around their necks and transform them into lanterns. They hung in the branches, glowing with tea lights. Under the deepening violet sky, the effect was magical.

Guests began to arrive in ones and twos, wine was poured, foil peeled off platters, and someone turned up the volume on a Blondie tune. The yard filled with a sea of neighbors and friends, journalism colleagues, people from other periods and places in our lives. I spied a friend from childhood summers, another couple who had flown in from California.

Our two older children, ages nine and six, wove through the crowd, proudly passing trays of finger food, eliciting wide smiles and animated praise from the adults. Nestled in an infant front pack, my daughter Nora stirred against my chest.

In the far corner of the yard, my husband cradled her

twin sister, Claire, in an identical baby carrier. Both girls slept soundly, soothed by the proximity of our heartbeats, the perpetual motion, and the white noise of a rocking party. Born by surrogate one month earlier, at the very end of my thirty-ninth year, the twins were our miracle babies.

"I am beyond happy," I thought as I gazed around at the swell of friends. In that moment, everything about my life was solidly in an upward trajectory. I felt earth-mothery in my thin dress and leather sandals, incandescent and content as I hugged my sleeping infant. Darting around clusters of guests like a hummingbird, I had the sense of simultaneously standing at an epicenter and being poised for a new beginning.

I caught Bob's eye, and the look my husband and I exchanged needed no translation. A flush of love burned me straight through. Undiluted joy. We were blessed, rootless gypsies at heart, ready for our next adventure. When we were married twelve years before, we made a pact to value travel and experience over the accumulation of things, and we had done exactly that. It was the credo for how we wanted to live and so far, we'd been true to it.

Nora arched her tiny back, stretched out a pebble-size fist, and mewled in the front pack. I placed my palm across her little bottom and my heart turned over. Love crackled through me, circulating like electricity. "I am forty," I thought, still testing how the number sounded, weighty and formidable, both young and wise. The perfect age.

I understood that real life didn't follow a script, that there were many things beyond our control. But there was a part of me, sprinkled with magical thinking and a sense of justice, that wanted to believe if we loved well and worked hard, if we put our shoulders into the life we'd made together, we'd be rewarded with mostly good things, that we'd be shielded from tragedy.

I was at Disney World when the president of ABC News called to tell me that Bob had been critically injured by a roadside bomb while reporting on the war in Iraq. His army convoy had been attacked; an IED (improvised explosive device) detonated twenty-five feet from his vehicle.

It was early morning in Florida, and my children were still asleep. I only remember fragments of the conversation. "Shrapnel to the brain," he said. "Unsure if he will make it through surgery." As I held the phone to my ear, the planet stopped spinning. My heart cracked inside my chest, a physical, splintering pain, the exact opposite of joy.

I flew to Germany and sat by my husband's bed in the military hospital, leaning over his comatose body as machines beeped and whooshed, alternating between numbness and blind hope. "Give me a sign that you hear me," I pleaded. There was no response for thirty-six days.

In the months before they replaced part of his skull with a plastic piece, I could not bring myself to touch the top of Bob's head. As the wife of a war correspondent, I had occasionally contemplated widowhood. But not once had I ever considered disability. Now his brain was broken, injured. I fell in love with that brain. I did not want to think about what might be changed inside, what might change us.

When Bob finally woke, very suddenly one day, determined to drive his recovery, my entire aperture on the world had been rearranged. I understood, with clarity, that there was no perfect age, no guaranteed charmed stretch of adulthood. I had envisioned my forties as a mostly joyous, jumbled combination of mothering, marriage, work, and play. Of course there would be challenges, but we had four healthy children, we loved our work, both sets of our parents were still active. Wasn't this decade supposed to be the wonderful gooey, marshmallow center of life?

The naive part of me had been taught that nothing is promised. Life was, indeed, short and it was the people you loved who really mattered. The immediacy of the moment was our only guarantee. All I had during the weeks and months of Bob's recovery was the present, and I needed to learn how to live there. My desires were suddenly very simple. I wanted my husband to continue improving, to recover.

And he did. But as Bob's brain gradually healed, my father's brain was quietly failing. After years of subtle decline, his Alzheimer's diagnosis arrived in the wake of Bob's injury. My mother and I were traveling in different directions, on the same continuum.

During Bob's injury and long recovery, my mother had kicked into gear, bucking me up, consoling and soothing on the phone with unconditional, maternal love. Navigating each stage of my father's disease, she modeled devotion and dignity in ways that were humbling. These were different skills than I had valued as a girl, aspirational ones. Her steady, practiced patience in the small spaces and endless time zones of caregiving was a balm to all of us.

Just shy of a decade after Bob's injury, my father passed away. His death granted my mother freedom from caregiving. But something deep and habitual had been lost, too. She was a swan without a mate.

During my visits to her in Boston now, as I sit, patiently

answering questions and describing each family member's activities, I am often struck by the differences in our worlds. Each time, my mother is newly incredulous as I tick off the cities I will travel to for work, the continents Bob was reporting from, the miracle of his recovery. I know that she is proud of the equality in my marriage, the way I could walk out the door and expect that my husband would have the back end and how he could do the same. The runway of my mother's life had offered only a short list of options. But my own path had provided so many more possibilities; opportunities that have resulted in an electric, patchwork quilt of a life. Yet it never seemed she felt cheated, in ways I might have if I were her.

"I worry about you." Her eyes crinkled with kindly concern as I leaned in for a last hug, preparing for the drive home. The few rooms in her small apartment were white and devoid of possessions. A photo of her nine grandchildren, lined up like stair steps on our family lakefront dock, sat framed in the living room. Her world was now as tiny and protective as a cocoon.

"My little multitasker," she added. "You do so much." At eighty-four, she has uttered this same phrase for decades. By now, I have accepted it as a form of love, although my younger self still hears the judgment. She beamed with a mother's pride watching how each of her daughters spun their way through an uncertain world; constructed lives and careers; raised families, navigated the tricky shoals of marriage, relationships, and health scares.

Throughout my forties and now into my fifties, the middle-ish place in my life, I have come to view my mother in a softer, more forgiving light. When I beam her accomplishments through the prism of experience, my former, judgmental perspective refracts and expands. My mother has so many additional angles and gradations than I could have ever imagined as a girl. The deep reserves of her patience, quiet strength, perseverance, and unself-conscious competence had eluded my younger self.

The decades ahead still feel bright with possibility to me, but the light is dappled, more diffuse. Time bombs explode all around us: marriages fail, relationships in malaise; illness and diagnoses choose randomly, without explanation. And while Bob has recovered miraculously, his injury makes him more susceptible to a host of neurological conditions later in life. If something should happen to my husband, I hope that I can be as fierce as my mother, as strong and true, as devoted as she was to my father in his final years.

In my mind I am still forty, still a young mother, that

woman at the backyard birthday party with her newborn twins, surrounded by family and friends. But time is a sneaky thief. I see it captured in the snapshots of my life, the way I catch a reflection in a plate-glass window and realize, a fraction of a second later, that it is *me*. The horizon line simply rearranges itself as we approach.

I feel this most acutely watching my teenaged daughters as they navigate the world and begin to make their place. Last spring, I observed them standing in front of the bathroom mirror, getting ready for junior prom. Spaghetti strap gowns, curling irons, and eyeliner gradually transformed my babies into sophisticated beauties. "How had we gotten here so fast?" I kept thinking. In one more year they would leave the nest.

"Mom, can we use some of your nice face cream?" Claire asked sweetly. She meant the expensive stuff, my Crème de la Mer, an indulgence I allowed myself in the quest for eternal youth.

"Sure," I said, unscrewing the top and demonstrating how to apply it in little dabs.

I thought about my mother's dressing table when I was a girl, those extravagant beauty purchases so many decades earlier. I understood now what those luxurious creams, that precious bottle of Youth Dew had meant to her, how in some small way they had saved her. They had gotten her through something, a period she had needed to endure.

Observing my girls during these milestone moments, I am often struck by the overarching questions, the ones that will not be answered for years, if ever. What parts of my life will my daughters appropriate? Will they reject the often harried way I straddle home and career, one eye always planning ahead, preparing contingencies? Maybe they will choose my mother's life instead, always physically present, closer to home. Have I made it all look too easy? Too crazed and unattractive? Have I offered them a realistic picture of how difficult it can be? Or have I been, at times, too honest, too exasperated and overwhelmed, or not enough?

The options my daughters have, the choices they will need to make, are both fearsome and awesome, in equal measure. I only hope that, like my mother, I have given them my best stuff, taught them by example that as we move through the years, we are built to bounce, to be resilient, even as we bend from the weight of what we carry.

I have come to understand in midlife that my mother and I are not, as I had once thought, so dissimilar. We have both chosen love and family, we have nurtured and evolved, been delighted and disappointed in different ways. We have each tried to appreciate beauty, to move through the world with grace while accepting our own limitations. And while our choices might have been different, I can see now how my life has grown out of hers, the way a branch grows from the trunk of the tree.

15

Quantum Physics for Birthdays

TAFFY BRODESSER-AKNER

Here's a short physics lecture before we get down to it: you have to look at time not like an emotional mess, but like a scientist. Both emotional messes and scientists have valid points on time—and on age, which is the specific thing that time leads to—and both are people whose days are numbered, so they have a real stake in the thinking. (And, of course, some scientists are emotional messes, but that's a subject for another time.) It's just that it doesn't help to look at all this if you're too emotional, because the emotion—the panic, wistfulness—is not going to help you. It might cloud the other things that happen with time; it might cloud the way good things happen when you age. So please be a scientist so that by the end of this conversation, you have a shot at understanding that all of this is good news.

18 Years

The second half of life will go by a million times faster and harder than the first, not just because every moment is precious or whatever, but for a practical reason: physics again.

When you're in grade school, let's say, and it feels like social studies is taking forever, even though it's only forty-five minutes long, that's because it *is* taking forever in terms of relative minutes you've been alive: if your only state of comparison is twelve years, say, then forty-five minutes is not really a small chunk of that. So you sit and you watch the second hand on the Seth Thomas clock tick and tick till—did it just tick backward?—somehow it ends, right about after you've been destroyed by it. This doesn't just apply to things you don't like. Remember the first day of camp? The first day of camp seemed like it lasted one hundred years, too, right? We'll call this Akner's theory of relativity.

Now take time in early adulthood. At eighteen, time has sped up slightly as you've cried with your classmates about this being the end of the beginning of life, but the anticipation that comes with entering adult life creates a Schrödinger's cat effect on time: Is it moving fast, or is it not? Is your youth dead or is it not? This perspective is affected most severely by the excitement that comes along with it, which will be notably absent later when, as I said, your life is halfway done. But at eighteen, though time has sped up from the time you were twelve, it is not yet moving significantly faster than any other time you could remember.

I spent my eighteenth birthday in Israel, on a gap year. I'd become the local drinking age that night, so my friends and I went to dinner and a disco. There was this one club where there was a DJ, but he played the same set list every night. We stayed out past when the buses were stopped, and we were aware of this. The night, like all the all-nights of that time of my life, stretched out and out, so that we had a feeling of gods about us each of these times, even if nothing happened. We would stop our dancing for a minute and, panting, say things like, "Can you believe this?" and "This is like so major." ("Major" was our "epic.") I had the feeling that night, as "Smells Like Teen Spirit" played, that my life could be a special thing. I knew that I was at the beginning of something. I was aware that that was the best place to be. At home, where my family was very religious and so was my high school, I watched TV in order to understand how secular humans interacted so that I'd know how to do that once I got out. I watched *A Different World* so that I knew how college students related to one another.

But I also watched *Thirtysomething* so that I could know, when it was time, how adults in a marriage should relate. My parents were divorced; my mother and stepfather were Israeli, so I couldn't understand most of their interaction. The thing I knew from watching *Thirtysomething* was that young adulthood—meaning, the age I was exactly now as I danced to that song—was where you wanted to be. You would look back on it forever. Nobody could tell me youth was great. People told me all my life that I was lucky to be a kid, and I had no qualms about saying, "Are you fucking kidding me?" Being a child was the worst. You were all potential, and people buzzed around you not with pleasure but with nervousness. What would you be? How might you let them down? How might they not be fulfilling some task of theirs that would enable your success? It was too much.

So at twenty-one, I knew that I was filled with potential, still, but now whatever happened to me would be my own doing. I was responsible. It was all ahead of me. That's what I had going for me. That night, after they played "Hotel California," which we knew was the last song, we crawled out onto the cobblestone streets where the disco was incongruously placed and watched the sky brighten before dawn and the streets fill with the sounds of trucks and their deliveries. The night had lasted all night. I had a million of these ahead of me.

27 Years

At twenty-seven, time is now moving at a completely reasonable rate. It is perhaps the only time in your life this will be true, but again, you don't know about the nature of time. You think time isn't quite so slow anymore because you have a reasonable amount of autonomy. There's not social studies class anymore. There's no Seth Thomas clock.

Work lasts how long work should. The weekend lasts just in time for you to conduct yourself as a twenty-seven-year-old should, recover from that conduct, go back to work. A night watching TV can last forever. A night with friends is only slightly shorter for its social momentum.

I didn't notice that the nights were no longer lasting as long as they used to. My life was no longer about the future, but about the very, very micro-present. There was a guy at work, and I fell in love with him in a way that made me finally understand why poets wrote and singers sang. Every feeling

I had about him infused every red blood cell I had until he was the machine that propelled me through a day. He broke my heart a thousand ways. The first five hundred were him teaching me he would do that. The next five hundred were me not being able to extricate myself. Finally, I met another guy—a wonderful guy—and I forced myself into a very comfortable relationship with him so that the relationship with the second man could become methadone to get me off the first man. Everything hurt in those days. There were no rejections that I could abide. There were no sinking feelings that I thought would ever go away. Everything needed immediate treatment. Heartbreak lasted too long still.

On my twenty-eighth birthday, my boyfriend, the second one, threw me a party at my own behest. But my birthday is problematic. It comes on a day that is also usually a very important baseball day. Because of this, my boyfriend threw my party at a sports bar. When I walked in, it was a pivotal moment of the game, and nobody at my party was allowed to greet me or say hello or happy birthday. We all waited for this game to be over. If you ever want to feel like time has really slowed down, watch a baseball game. You could live forever waiting for a baseball game to end. Someone at my party asked my boyfriend what he was getting me for my birthday. The next morning, we woke up and he told me he thought that was a rude question. I asked him why. He said he hadn't thought about it yet. But my birthday was yesterday, I said. He said he was thinking, he was thinking. I told him that this was over. Not because of the birthday present or the party— well, not just because of it. It was time. I had spent two years with him. Two years like I had spent two years on everything. I was twenty-eight. Time had been so generous, but twenty-eight had come a little quicker than I expected. It led to twenty-nine, which was the official age my mother always pretended to be. It had to be that time's generosity was running out.

35 Years

Your thirties are where you pick up the most speed. I was married to a wonderful man by thirty. I had a son at thirty-two and another at thirty-four. I had worked out the time very well: I had both kids before doctors would need to recommend high-risk testing, and I did this on purpose. I had a career now, writing, and when I dropped the children off with their babysitter, I couldn't fathom how little time I actually had alone. When I would pick them up, time slowed down again. Babies do that, not necessarily in a good way.

They slow down time enough so that you have time to think of the time, so you're basically back in social studies. Only now you hate yourself for it because you're supposed to hate social studies; you're not supposed to be wary of the time when you're with your kids.

On my rare nights out, and even during those babysitter hours, I learned to move with high efficiency and economy of motion. I learned to make decisions based on the fact that the time would go faster than I thought and then it would be over. I would only go to movies that would verifiably change my life. I would only travel all the way to the other side of town if the meal was going to profoundly alter my universe. But movies and meals and all the other pleasures of autonomous time: they were good because you knew the time was ending, but they were never good enough to justify the time. Your thirties are a frenzy.

In my thirties, I saw the dawn again, but it was a sign of misery. It was a sign I'd been up with children, or up worrying about my career or my future. When a dark sky began to glow through my window, and I was in my glider, or on my couch, or just staring out the window from my bed, I became filled with dread, and mostly I was confused: How did the night go by so quickly?

40 Years

Okay, here we are: life is half over and we'll never be able to appreciate how young we are because in the moments when we're considering time, we're older than we've ever been. Like now. And then now. And then now. See how it works?

With all this in mind, what do you do? How do you proceed? Well, if we've learned anything in our endless and yet very quick time here, it's that we proceed no matter what. And that's ultimately what getting older is about. It's that time happens no matter what you're doing with it. You learn to look life in the eye and realize you're only seeing a tiny cross section of it, if you can hold that concept in your head. That can be bad—it can depress you to know all that history—but it can also free you in a way.

On the day I turned forty, I woke up to a flurry of Facebook messages that said things like "Happy 29th birthday!" and "Age is just a number!" Forty is a number; it's a number of years you use to indicate to your doctor how used up your body is. But, just forty! Not bad, right? I thought getting old would be gradual; it had been so far. My Facebook friends, however, had a certain cutoff for youth. Facebook did, too. I was suddenly being advertised eye creams and coffins—no shit, coffins, too. Today was the day we would start pretending I was young, since by all metrics available I no longer was. Age is just a number yes. But it's a number that indicates just how used up your body is.

Fuck this, I thought, and I shut off my phone. Your forties dull you. I'm not saying that to be cruel or a downer. But this isn't a moisturizer commercial; I'm not going to tell you things that aren't true. Your forties dull you, and so time is going by quicker than it ever was, and you are now keenly aware that it will be going even faster a minute from now. But the way that that bothers you now is a little duller. Is "dull" bringing you down? Let's use "mellow" instead. In your forties, the way you were set afire by everything changes. You are now slightly more *mellow*.

I got up and put on my tennis skirt and checked movie times. I drove forty minutes to see a movie that I'd wanted to see and that was about to leave theaters. The movie was terrible and felt like four hours. (Was it? Wikipedia has its running time at 2 hours and 1 minute, but, again, time is different on your birthday.) I called up the tennis club near my house and asked if any of the instructors were available for a last-minute lesson. There was one guy who could do it, and when I got there, I told him it was my fortieth birthday, and he was very nice and polite about it—"It's never too late!"—even excited for me, but then he asked me the date, and I told him and he realized it was his wife's birthday also and he'd forgotten about it, and now he was very distracted. This lesson lasted longer than your average tennis lesson.

I went to pick my kids up from school, and in the car line I called the rock-climbing place near me and arranged for a private lesson for us three. We got to the rock-climbing place, and I climbed a very high wall, even though I was really afraid to because heights give me vertigo and existential compulsion dread. I got to the top and I rang the bell, and from beneath, my sons and the stoner who was operating my tenuous harness cheered for me. Forty! At forty, I do these things! At forty, I live right. At forty, I finally do what the email signatures have been beseeching me to do all these years: I dance like no one is watching; I am the change I want to see in the world; I consider the environment before printing. I have arrived! I've arrived right on time!

But then, I came down off the wall. We went to Chipotle on the way and ate tacos. We went home. My younger son threw a tantrum. My older son asked for screens. Ah, so forty would be exactly the same as thirty-nine and thirty-eight and thirty-seven. I would just be me, but at forty. At home, I looked in the mirror at the desert of my face. I have two dimples, the crowning glory of my head, and now, when I stopped smiling, they took a few more seconds before they disappeared into my cheeks. My hair was now too gray just for some highlights.

I still hadn't written a book. I will now officially never be young and hot. Maybe I'd get older and have some kind of Helen Mirren thing going on (I wouldn't, but also, does it ever occur to you that the Helen Mirren hotness conversation goes on with such a lack of subtly because it isn't true, and because we don't actually think old people are hot?), but I'd never be young and hot. It was not looking like I'd ever spend a year in Paris—how? How could I do that exactly? I will never get so good at tennis that someone would call me a great or good tennis player. That's the strangest thing about being as obsessed with time as I am. You can be acutely aware of it, you can watch it go by with the understanding that each minute leads to a deficit on the other end, but that doesn't ever spur you to action. It doesn't ever change who you actually are. Your mellowing changes your ambition a little; it makes you less upset about it. That in turn changes how you pursue things. That part of my fortieth birthday, when I realized this, lasted longer than any theory of time and space should allow.

I tried to summon a sense of accomplishment and relief. I had lived to forty! I had made it. I didn't want to pretend I was twenty-nine. I didn't even wish I was thirty-five. I could account for every day. I was proud of it. I had collected all those moments inside my body and I was here and in relatively good shape over all for it. I was happy to be here. I was never going to be hot, no, but on my fortieth birthday, I realized I could dispense with the idea that I ever have to think about anything as inane as hotness again. I was immediately alleviated of all the choices I made that I was still ambivalent about: how much to work, how many kids to have, whether or not I should get married in the first place. Those choices were made. Here I was. I looked at my youth as a thing that existed inside of a book with a beginning and a middle and an end, a thing with a leather cover that could close. I'd gotten married. I'd stayed married. I was a good sister and a good daughter. I was an okay wife and mother. I had children, two of them, and they were clean and healthy and on their way, enduring forty-five-minute social studies classes that felt like ten years. I had a career I was proud of. And yet, what was it all for? Who cared, now that I was forty?

40 years, 1 day

But. *But.* But on the day after my fortieth birthday, something shifted. That day was a regular day for me. I finished a story.

I edited another one. I went to the coffee place in town and I said to someone that I was forty now and that I had reached cultural irrelevance. It was a joke. When I was thirty-nine, she would have laughed. But now I was forty, and being forty is sad, so she told me she'd just read a story I'd written—how can I say I'm culturally irrelevant? I'm so culturally relevant! I wanted to correct her and tell her I was mostly kidding, but she was thirty-four. Turning forty is like childbirth. Read about it all you want, know you'll go through it, but you can't really explain it to someone who has not yet gone through the looking glass.

That night, I sent my children to bed. I sat outside. I had a house now, and a place to sit, and nothing contented me more than knowing they were asleep and I was still awake. I was stealing some time, always, even as I was being told that my time was up. Those two or three hours that I was awake after them went by like you couldn't believe.

At forty, the two hours my children are in bed while I'm still awake are a blip. Two hours is nothing. It's a sigh; it's a yawn. It's applying nail polish to your toes and waiting while it dries. It's trying to understand how to use Venmo. A movie feels like a flash, and a year will (and already does) feel like a month. A weekday is about the time it takes to figure out dinner and look up an exercise schedule and decide not to go. A weekday is the amount of time it takes to go to a makeup counter and have a saleswoman try to say as nicely and delicately as she can (which is not nicely and delicately at all) that the area beneath your eyes is as dry and desolate as a sponge, and with similar topography. Forty-five minutes is one phone call to the orthopedist to look into your knee problem. A weekend vanishes while you're planning it.

But here's the thing: time was moving quickly whether or not I consented to it. I had somehow thought I could game the system if I noticed it, if I could call out time and yell at it for not behaving. But I couldn't. Time was going quickly because it was supposed to now. Time was going quickly because I wasn't meandering anymore. I knew how to use it.

I decided to stop thinking of these things. It wasn't helping. Age doesn't exist until we look directly at it. You can remind yourself of this when you're hopeless about time passing, but then you're looking directly at it again and you're back to square one. You should only care about getting older if you aren't moving every day toward the maximal expression of the life you were hoping for.

So take a minute. Forty is a rest stop in which you can pause to hold something in your hand and examine it from all sides, but just as quickly, because it's all suddenly moving so fast, you let it go. Which is a good thing, because the modern woman, at least the kind who is reading a book of essays about turning forty, is faced with a conundrum at forty: How can you be this dissatisfied when you have so much? How can you be this satisfied when you have so little? Ask yourself this, and then know you won't find an answer. Decide that it is okay to not have an answer. It is also okay to forget the question.

That night after my fortieth birthday, I sat outside, and the New Jersey sky began to reveal itself in a glow that you could mistake for the dawn. It's the dusk. Man, I have fallen in love with the dusk. That's the thing. If you allow yourself to stop living in the gloaming of your childhood, you will stop hating yourself for all the ways you no longer love the dawn. You will now celebrate every dusk you have. You will not believe how beautiful the dusk can be.

The quote or mantra that most speaks to me about this moment in my life is . . .

Jessica Lahey

"I decided that I would make my life my argument."

—Albert Schweitzer

Sloane Crosley

"A genius is the one most like himself."

—Thelonious Monk

Veronica Chambers

"My mission in life is not merely to survive, but to thrive; and to do so with some passion, some compassion, some humor, and some style."

—Maya Angelou

KJ Dell'Antonia

"Maybe it is all quite simple. We are born, we experience some happiness and sadness, and we die. That is all."

—Patricia De Martelaere

Sophfronia Scott

"I have the nerve to walk my own way, however hard, in my search for reality, rather than climb upon the rattling wagon of wishful illusions."

—Zora Neale Hurston

Acknowledgments

This book wouldn't exist without two wonderful, 40-ish women: Christine Pride and Brettne Bloom. Working with them has been a joy and a privilege. I owe them both enormous thanks for their generous shepherding of this book and, equally, for the inspiration they are to me personally.

The writers who share their stories and reflections here are the heart and soul of this book. The pieces make me laugh, they make me cry, they make me shake my head with profound identification. In short, they do what great writing does: they make me feel less alone and connect me to the wide world around me. It has been my honor to work with these artists.

Thank you also to my friends, especially those of whom

I write in this book's introduction. It's impossible to adequately acknowledge those peers who are sharing this rich, marvelous, and exhausting decade with me. For more than twenty years I've been grateful to feel your days thrumming beside mine, and your good humor, unceasing support, and deep wisdom has enriched my life more than I can say.

Finally, thank you to my family. Mum and Hilary, you are respectively an example of and a compatriot in the art of midlife womanhood, in all of its complexities, demands, and joys. Matt, you're my ground zero and my biggest supporter, and I can't think of anyone I'd rather be walking this path with. Grace and Whit, you're the reason I get up in the morning. I know that having a mother who works full-time and writes part-time means I'm a little more distracted and a little less engaged than you sometimes wish. Thank you for your patience and your love, and for all the ways you've made me aware of life's bittersweet beauty. And, Dad, so recently gone, thank you. I'm grateful that you saw me into my forties and I'm grateful you knew of this collection. I loved being your daughter for forty-three years, and I'll miss you all the days of my life.

Contributors

KATE BOLICK's first book, the bestselling *Spinster: Making a Life of One's Own*, was a *New York Times* Notable Book of 2015. A contributing editor for the *Atlantic*, Bolick teaches writing in New York University's graduate program in Cultural Reporting & Criticism, and hosts "Touchstones at The Mount," an annual interview series at Edith Wharton's country estate in Lenox, Massachusetts. She lives in Brooklyn.

TAFFY BRODESSER-AKNER is a features writer for the *New York Times* Arts and the *New York Times Magazine*. Her novel, *Fleishman Is in Trouble*, will be published in 2019 by Random House.

VERONICA CHAMBERS is a prolific author and journalist best known for her critically acclaimed memoir *Mama's Girl*; the young adult novel *The Go-Between*; and the *New York Times* bestseller *Yes, Chef*, which was coauthored with chef Marcus Samuelsson. She is the editor of *The Meaning of Michelle: 16 Writers on the Iconic First Lady and How Her Journey Inspires Our Own*. She was a culture writer at *Newsweek* and an editor at the *New York Times Magazine*. She teaches creative writing and journalism, most recently as a lecturer in the Earth Systems Program in the School of Earth, Energy, and Environmental Sciences at Stanford.

SLOANE CROSLEY is the author of *I Was Told There'd Be Cake*, a finalist for the Thurber Prize; *How Did You Get This Number*; and the novel *The Clasp*. Her third book of essays, *Look Alive Out There*, is out now. She is a frequent contributor to the *New York Times* and a contributing editor at *Vanity Fair*. She lives in Manhattan.

MEGHAN DAUM is the author of four books, most recently *The Unspeakable: And Other Subjects of Discussion*. She is also the editor of *Selfish, Shallow, and Self-Absorbed: Sixteen Writers on the Decision Not to Have Kids*. A longtime opinion columnist for the *Los Angeles Times*, she now writes the Egos column for the *New York Times Book Review*.

Five years of editing the Motherlode column for the *New York Times* taught KJ DELL'ANTONIA this: family can be a source of joy, not stress. Her reporting and research on parental happiness led to her book *How to Be a Happier Parent*, and she continues to explore that topic in both nonfiction and fictional forms. She is also the cohost of the popular podcast *#AmWriting with Jess and KJ*. She lives in New Hampshire with her husband, four children, and assorted horses, chickens, dogs, and cats.

A born and bred New Yorker, JILL KARGMAN, age forty-three, is the creator, writer, producer, and star of the scripted comedy *Odd Mom Out* in which Ms. Kargman played a satirical version of herself navigating the hilarity of raising children on the Upper East Side of Manhattan. Kargman attended the Spence School, the Taft School, and Yale University. After graduating, and working for magazines, television, and movies, Kargman began writing novels to give her more flexibility to be home with her three children, Sadie, Ivy, and Fletch. She is a *New York Times* bestselling author of multiple books.

She made her Café Carlyle debut in January 2017 with her sold out show, *Stairway to Cabaret*, singing heavy metal songs cabaret-style. Kargman hosts her hour-long biweekly radio show on SiriusXM, channel 102, Radio Andy. She is also a performer with the Upright Citizens Brigade improvisational and sketch comedy group. Kargman recently made an appearance in her first Hollywood studio movie, *A Bad Moms Christmas*, and she is currently working with Seth Meyers on a reboot of *The Munsters* for NBC.

JULIE KLAM is the *New York Times* bestselling author of five books. She also writes for the *New York Times* and the *Washington Post* and the small handful of magazines that haven't folded. She lives in New York City with her daughter, dogs, and boyfriend (though she wishes there was a better word for boyfriend at her age).

JESSICA LAHEY is a teacher, writer, and mom. She writes about education, parenting, and child welfare for the *Atlantic*, Vermont Public Radio, and the *New York Times*, and is the author of the *New York Times* bestselling book *The Gift of Failure: How the Best Parents Learn to Let Go So Their Children Can Succeed*. She is a member of the Amazon Studios Thought Leader Board and wrote the educational curriculum for

Amazon Kids' *The Stinky & Dirty Show*. Lahey earned a BA in comparative literature from the University of Massachusetts and a JD with a concentration in juvenile and education law from the University of North Carolina School of Law. She lives in New Hampshire with her husband and two sons and teaches high school English and writing in Vermont.

CATHERINE NEWMAN is the author of the memoirs *Catastrophic Happiness* and *Waiting for Birdy*, as well as the middle-grade novel *One Mixed-Up Night* and the blog *Ben & Birdy*. She is also the etiquette columnist for *Real Simple* and a regular contributor to the *New York Times*; *O, The Oprah Magazine*; the *Boston Globe*; and many other publications. She lives in Amherst, Massachusetts, with her family.

SUJEAN RIM is a freelance illustrator. Her clients include Tiffany & Co., UNAIDS, and Victoria's Secret. Rim is also a children's book author. She lives with her husband and son in New York.

JENA SCHWARTZ is the author of three collections, most recently *Why I Was Late for Our Meeting*. Her work has appeared on numerous blogs and websites, including *On Being*, *Full Grown People*, *Mamalode*, and *The Manifest-Station*. She works as a writing coach and group facilitator and lives in Amherst, Massachusetts, with her wife and two kids. Visit her at www.jenaschwartz.com.

SOPHFRONIA SCOTT lives in Sandy Hook, Connecticut, where she continues to fight a losing battle against the weeds in her flowerbeds. A former editor for *Time* and *People*, she holds a BA in English from Harvard and an MFA in writing, fiction, and creative nonfiction from Vermont College of Fine Arts. Scott is the author of two novels, *All I Need to Get By* and *Unforgivable Love*, as well as an essay collection, *Love's Long Line*, and a spiritual memoir, *This Child of Faith: Raising a Spiritual Child in a Secular World*, cowritten with her son, Tain Gregory. She teaches creative writing at Regis University's Mile High MFA and Bay Path University's MFA in Creative Nonfiction. Her website is www.Sophfronia.com.

ALLISON WINN SCOTCH is the *New York Times* bestselling author of seven novels, including *Between Me and You*, *In Twenty Years*, *The Theory of Opposites*, and *Time of My Life*. She lives in Los Angeles with her family and their dogs.

LEE WOODRUFF is the author of two nonfiction memoirs, including the *New York Times* bestselling *In an Instant*, which she cowrote with her journalist husband after his roadside bomb injury in Iraq. Her third bestselling book, *Those We Love Most*, is her first novel. She has written numerous essays and articles over her five decades (and change) and is extremely flattered to be included with the much younger authors in this collection. Woodruff is the mother of four mostly grown children and is married to a man who is still a kid at heart. They currently live in Westchester County, New York, and are dreaming about their next extended adventure once the dog dies.